A PLUME BOOK

ROCK STAR BABYLON

JON HOLMES is an award-winning writer, broadcaster and comedian whose writing has appeared in *The Guardian, The Times, The Sunday Times* and *Time Out* (London). He proudly holds the record for the largest ever fine for taste and decency offenses in British broadcasting history, achieved with his on-air game of "Swearing Radio Hangman for the Under 12s."

ROCK
STAR
BABYLON

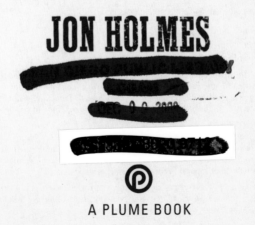

Outrageous Rumors, Legends, and Raucous
True Tales of Rock and Roll Icons

JON HOLMES

A PLUME BOOK

PLUME
Published by the Penguin Group
Penguin Group (USA) Inc., 375 Hudson Street, New York, New York 10014, U.S.A. •
Penguin Group (Canada), 90 Eglinton Avenue East, Suite 700, Toronto, Ontario, Canada
M4P 2Y3 (a division of Pearson Penguin Canada Inc.) • Penguin Books Ltd., 80 Strand,
London WC2R 0RL, England • Penguin Ireland, 25 St. Stephen's Green, Dublin 2, Ireland
(a division of Penguin Books Ltd.) • Penguin Group (Australia), 250 Camberwell Road,
Camberwell, Victoria 3124, Australia (a division of Pearson Australia Group Pty. Ltd.) •
Penguin Books India Pvt. Ltd., 11 Community Centre, Panchsheel Park, New Delhi – 110
017, India • Penguin Group (NZ), 67 Apollo Drive, Rosedale, North Shore 0632, New
Zealand (a division of Pearson New Zealand Ltd.) • Penguin Books (South Africa) (Pty.)
Ltd., 24 Sturdee Avenue, Rosebank, Johannesburg 2196, South Africa

Penguin Books Ltd., Registered Offices: 80 Strand, London WC2R 0RL, England

Published by Plume, a member of Penguin Group (USA) Inc. Previously published in a
Michael Joseph edition, under the title *Status Quo and the Kangaroo,* in Great Britain.

First American Printing, July 2008
10 9 8 7 6 5 4 3 2 1

 REGISTERED TRADEMARK—MARCA REGISTRADA

CIP data is available.
ISBN 978-0-452-28941-3

Printed in the United States of America

For Mum, Dad, Kelda and Vicky

Contents

Introduction   xiii

Status Quo and the Kangaroo   1

Almond Surprise   5

Girls Aloud Fought the Law and the Law
    Won   9

James Brown Has Powerful Testicles,
    Given to Him by the Government   13

Puff Party   16

Not a Well(er) Man   20

It's the Wrong Dave Stewart, Gromit   24

Shit Hot   26

Wet Wet Dry (Ice)   31

A Man Called Jim Webb   35

Holy Pigs   38

Heaven Is a Place on Eargghhth   41

Contents

Hey, You, Get off of My Pie   44

I Warn You, This Is Quite Unpleasant   47

Manic Street Pɹɘɒɔɥɘɿƨ   51

The Baker Street Irregularity   54

Boys Who Like Girls   58

The Adventures of Brinsley Schwarz   61

The Bones Is Mine   65

Who's Gonna Drive You Home . . . ?   68

Pink Sabbath   72

Lost in Transfusion   75

Mercury Rising   78

Oh What a Feeling, When You're Stuck up
in the Ceiling   82

My Heart Will Go On, but I Won't   86

The Devil in Mr. Johnson   91

The Best to You Each Morning   94

No Sleep 'til Dresden   97

Fleetwood Crack   101

Blondie: Portrait of a Serial Killer   106

Papa's Got a Brand-New Bag   110

Games Without Frontiers   114

Too Young to Live, Too Fat to Fly   118

'I Said No Squeaks!'   121

Contents

Bring Me a Gun, Mr. Piano Man   123

New Sensation   126

One (Pissed) Man Went to Mow   129

The Myths and Legends of King Rick and
    the Knights of the Round Table   133

Toxic Rock Syndrome   136

Simply the Bezst   139

Billy, Don't Be a Hero   142

Spinal Twat   145

Motley Spüe   148

By Royal Appointment   151

Snyder Remarks   155

Always on My Dad   157

When Pop Stars Divorce   161

Trying to Get Blood out of a Stone   164

Taking Libertines   167

Stairway to Hell   172

Jaz Mag   176

'Chute Me, I'm Only the Piano Player   180

Holding Back the Beers   183

A Fine Time   187

That Man Called Jim Webb Again   189

One-Armed Band Git   191

Contents

Chuck Up   194

Little White (Stripes) Lies   196

Dear Satan . . .   198

Curiosity Time   202

Born to Canoe   205

'Leave It, Omar, He's a Raspberry'   209

Where Eagles Fear to Tread   213

Private Dancer   218

Honestly, Pop Stars Today . . .   221

Dude (Looks Like a Cokehead)   225

Fall from Grace   228

You Give Accountancy a Bad Name   232

Pavarotti Goes to the Toilet   236

Queen Elton of John   237

Pete Townshend Strikes Again? (Or
   Rather, His Cat Does)   240

Dinner for Three   244

Johnny B. Bad   247

Ryder on the Storm   250

Eatin' the Blues   253

Ozzy Osbourne and the Exploding Mouse   255

He'll Be Coming Round the Mountain   258

One Final KISS   262

Contents

Endpiece   265
Further Reading   266
Acknowledgments   267

Introduction

'When the legend becomes truth, print the legend.'
John Ford

I think, probably, that legendary, be-ponytailed, waist-coat rockers Status Quo are quite possibly the only band in the world ever to have put the word 'margarita' into a UK Top 10 hit. How fitting then that up to ten of those very drinks had been consumed on the night that the idea for this book was born.

We were in the pub and, to misquote Pirandello, we were six characters in search of a pointless conversation. The jukebox was playing Van Halen's seminal classic 'Jump' and thus the conversation drifted like a bass player's concentration toward the story of Van Halen's rider—that long list of requests provided by bands to venues regarding their backstage requirements. We all knew, of course, of the story in which Van Halen once asked for a bowl of M&Ms with all the blue (or brown) ones taken out, but soon stories began to flow as fast as a cliché involving flowing beer. How we laughed at the idea that Iggy Pop once asked for seven dwarves, that J.Lo's coffee must only be stirred counterclockwise or that, wherever she goes, Mariah Carey always insists on a horse whisperer.

Another drink and the chat veered toward our favorite rock 'n' roll myths. The usual suspects emerged: Ozzy's bat snack, Mama Cass choking on a sandwich, Marilyn Manson starring in TV's *The Wonder Years* when he was young and Led Zeppelin sharing a fish with a groupie in such an original way that you certainly wouldn't find it in a Rick Stein cookbook.

But then someone told the story of Status Quo and the Kangaroo and the idea for this collection of stories and apocryphal tales from rock's highway to hell hewn roughly into the shape of a book was born.

Between its covers you will find both classic and perhaps lesser-known rock 'n' roll myths, paraphrased pop stories and terrifying, tawdry tales destined to be passed down from generation to generation as fact. Even though I'm legally obliged to point out at this time that some of them may not be. In the spirit of the excellent gossip website Popbitch and the fact that I'm indebted to musicians, journalists, DJs, writers and their potentially libelous (yet anonymous) mouths, I will leave you to decide which is which.

These stories were out there, so now they're in here, all lovingly annotated and remarked upon as we go along—sort of like a DVD commentary in written form. Get used to footnotes, you're going to need them.[1] These rock 'n' roll fables come from the road, from backstage, from the studio, from the bars, the hotels and most importantly from the hearts and minds of those about to and/or who have rock(ed). And for that, we salute them.

And yes, I know 'apocryphals' isn't a real word.

Jon Holmes, Los Angeles, 2006[2]

---

1. Like this.

2. Actually, at home in Canterbury, Kent, England, but that's not as glamorous in rock terms.

ROCK STAR
BABYLON

Status Quo and the Kangaroo

It's the mid-1980s and, having been busy rockin' all over the world and opening Live Aid,[1] the mighty denimed and ponytailed combo that are Status Quo find themselves on tour travelling between cities through the vast, scorching, bleached desert of the Australian outback. All was going well aboard the tour bus (drinking, smoking, swapping amusing anecdotes about the time Francis Rossi's cocaine-flustered septum

---

1. You know. The starving Africans thing. The first one in 1985. Not to be confused with the 2005 Live 8 one with Mariah Carey onstage, crying salty tears onto the faces of poverty-stricken orphans.

fell out) until, in the middle of nowhere and 300 miles from the nearest town, it happened.

Yes, that was the moment that Status Quo hit a kangaroo.

In the ensuing face-off that was tour bus vs. marsupial, the 'roo, rather unsurprisingly, had fared least well and the band piled out to find that, sadly, the be-pouched creature's bouncing days were over.[2] It was then that they did what any self-respecting rock band would do. That's right, they dressed the dead kangaroo in a denim jacket, a pair of sunglasses and a bandana and lined up with it to have their photo taken.

It was at this point that things went a bit wrong. Startled by the flash,[3] the actually-only-concussed kangaroo woke up, pushed the Quo aside with its meaty fists and bounded off into the desert.[4] It was soon lost

---

2. Unusually, its shiny coat and little kangaroo face hadn't been badly damaged and mangled like so many roadkill victims often are. Well they are, aren't they? Once, driving home from my girlfriend's parents' house in a V reg. Fiesta on Boxing Day evening in 1991, I turned a big rabbit inside out.

3. Yes, I know. Blazing sunshine and the flash went off. Sounds implausible until you remember that most point-and-shoot pocket cameras are part of the Borg Collective* and thus subject to some sort of overall sentient control outside our realm of understanding.

4. At about 37 mph, which is the top speed of a kangaroo. True fact. (Source: The Internet.)

* One for the Trekkies there.

over the horizon, still dressed like Lemmy out of Motorhead. How Status Quo laughed as they climbed back aboard the bus, thinking that the notion of a heavy metal kangaroo forever hopping off to the Bungle Bungles[5] was the funniest thing in rock history.[6] How they stopped laughing when they realized the bus ignition keys were in the pocket of the jacket.

Kangaroo 1, Status Quo 0.

---

5. The Bungle Bungles is a place in the Outback that used to get mentioned a lot in *Neighbours* back when Jim Robinson was alive. Helen Daniels used to go there to paint stuff, before her character's face went all lopsided and she died.

6. With the possible exception of the video for Robin George's 'Heartline' circa 1985.

Almond Surprise

Out of the dry ice–based mist of the British new romantic scene, an especially pointy 80s cheekboned face emerged. And it belonged to Marc Almond. Marc Almond was one half of Soft Cell, the synthesizer-wizard-based electrosexuals[1] with front-projecting hair who, until their breakthrough hit 'Tainted Love',[2] were jobbing DJs in some northern club or other.

---

1. Actually that could be libelous. They may not *both* have been synthesizer wizards.

2. A cover of the Gloria Jones hit of the 60s. I must admit that I didn't know that until today, but Google is my friend.

The back half of this pantomime cowlick was Dave Ball, whose job it was to stand around looking mustachioed.

This is a story that is destined to pass from generation to generation. A bit like the family silver, or chlamydia. That's right, this is the story of Marc Almond and the stomach pump. Now, if you know what's coming[3] then you may look away now. It stands to reason that you may already know this story of course because it's a classic, hence its inclusion.[4] And it goes like this:

The popular singer and homosexual Marc Almond goes to a party. The details of what sort of party it was aren't clear but I think we're safe to assume that it's not the sort of party that ends in cake and balloons.[5] It's an 80s pop party and he's probably hobnobbing[6] with Limahl, China Crisis and the Blow Monkeys.[7] Everyone's there, drinking Top Deck Shandy, nibbling on Space Invaders[8] and pickled onion Monster Munch

---

3. Ha. Haha.

4. That plus I'm not sure it's ever been told in written-down-in-a-book story form before. Probably with good reason as we're about to find out.

5. Actually, it may well have been. God only knows what was going on. There may even have been a rubber clown.

6. Again, who knows what was going on?

7. Again, who knows what was going on?

8. They were a corn-based crispy snack, presumably named after the popular computer game of the era.

and dancing to their own records, when suddenly Marc remembers that he's due onstage in Soho that very evening and is already late. He quickly gathers up his things[9] and heads for the door. He pauses to say hello, wave goodbye, to Kraftwerk, who are in the lounge playing Twister with Kenny Loggins, when suddenly it hits him. Disaster! He's about to leave, yet he hasn't even sucked anybody off.

At this point we'll gloss over the details. Suffice to say, satisfied, our party pal arrives at the gig just in time and takes to the stage. Then, half an hour in, he collapses, bringing the gig to an abrupt halt. Doctors quickly diagnose severe stomach pain and, what with him being a pop star and everything, assume that some sort of overdose is in progress and summon a stomach pump. And then they pump his stomach.

They were right. It *was* an overdose. Of sorts. From his stomach they removed a pint of semen. That's right, semen.[10] Mr. Almond had been admitted to the hospital with possibly the first-ever recorded case of sperm poisoning.[11]

---

9. Hair 'lacquer', eyeliner, thin tie.

10. In some versions of this tale it's not even human semen, but that of dogs and/or horses. And sometimes it's eight pints, not one. Now if that's the case, what sort of party must *that* have been? Presumably a swingers' one at a petting zoo.

11. It should be noted that Marc Almond categorically denies the whole sordid incident and I have to say that I believe him. In fact the self-same

Not a storyline that crops up often on *Holby City*, that one.[12]

story has, according to Snopes.com, been attributed over the years to Rod Stewart, Elton John, David Bowie, Mick Jagger, Andy Warhol, Jeff Beck, Jon Bon Jovi, the drummer out of Bon Jovi, the lead singer for New Kids on the Block, the Bay City Rollers (all of them), Alanis Morissette, Lil' Kim and Britney Spears. Fair enough, but there's no smoke without fire of course and the story had to begin somewhere, so let's think of who may have actually done it. My money is on Buddy Holly. I say that partly because he died under vaguely mysterious circumstances but mostly because he's dead and can't sue. There. I've said it. Marc Almond is innocent; Buddy Holly on the other hand was a veritable spunk bucket.

12. I've submitted a script to the producers, but they're not interested.

Girls Aloud Fought the Law
and the Law Won

Hahaha. Girls Aloud. Girls 'Allowed'. Girls Aloud. That's right, it's a pop pun. Hilarious. Girls 'Aloud' were forced together in 2002 for the reality shitcast that was ITV's *Popstars: The Rivals* and have done surprisingly well, given that they're still making records,[1] unlike, say, Gareth Gates[2] or Hear'say.

---

1. At time of writing.

2. At time of writing, a comeback is rumored. If it's happened by the time you're reading this, yay—get me and my insider knowledge. If we never hear from him again, simply forget I ever said anything. Just covering my bases.

Being a group of girls manufactured for the purposes of a TV show and having your every move, smile and topless magazine shoot for *Zoo* or *Nuts* magazine orchestrated to within an inch of your fixed smiles was, and probably still is,[3] some kind of living hell but with such acquiescence comes success. Sadly though, such success means that the gates of inevitable tabloid hell will eventually swing open in your direction. And so it was on one day early in 2003 when it nearly all came crashing down like a hippo in a child's hammock.

One of the band members—it was the drummer, Cheryl Tweedy[4]—was in a nightclub in Guildford, where she was simply doing what any girl of 19 would do.[5] She then went to the toilet, where on duty that night was a lady called Sophie Amogbokpa (39), a toilet

---

3. At time of writing.

4. Of course she's not the drummer. None of them are anything remotely bandlike. They are just pleasantly breasted pawns riding the music industry merry-go-round. They didn't really do anything to get there. It's simply their turn.

5. Binge drinking and gorging on dance. The whole band of course famously danced to 'the sound of the underground', which, given that the sound of the underground is just old trains screeching around bends and constant announcements about minding the gap, is a not unremarkable feat.

6. Quite what toilet 'assistants' of this nature are for is still a mystery so mysterious that even Dan Brown couldn't weave it into a plot. As far as I can see they're there to put a bit of squirty soap on your hands and then take a buck off you for doing it.

assistant.[6] What followed turned into an allegation, a court case, a racist slur and a fistfight. Not necessarily in that order. The tabloids gleefully reported that Cheryl Tweedy punched Ms. Amogbokpa in the face and let fly with what I imagine they called 'a torrent of racial abuse'. The other members of the band were aghast.[7] Ms. Amogbokpa was even aghaster, claiming to the newspapers:

I was shocked. I don't care how many number ones she's had,[8] if she was nobody, she shouldn't have said those things to me or hit me. I had done nothing to her and whoever gives me an eye like this should be punished.

She then claimed that Ms. Tweedy had been irate and called her 'a black bitch', saying she wanted to hit her again. The Girl Aloud was duly arrested and held for ten hours by the police. In court she denied any racial motivation and was duly acquitted of this charge but was instead convicted of assault, fined and shamed, and had to do 120 hours of community service. She then got married to the soccer player Ashley Cole, although it's not clear whether this was part of the punishment.

---

7. I'm not surprised. I mean, a pound? For a squirt of soap?

8. Do you think she meant this as a toilet joke? No. Me neither.

So, in conclusion, Girls Aloud star Cheryl Tweedy is a *violent* thug but not a racist one.[9] That's all right then.

---

9. Funnily enough, there's no mention of this in her biography on the official Girls Aloud website. It just mentions that, throughout her childhood, 'Cheryl Ann Tweedy' performed in a large number of model and fashion shows. She apparently also entered ballroom dancing competitions, sang, acted and did ballet. As a child, we're reliably informed, she won the following competitions: Boots Bonniest Baby, Mothercare Happy Faces Portrait competition, Best Looking Girl of Newcastle,* *The Evening Chronicle* 'Little Miss & Mister' and Most Attractive Girl at the Metro Centre.** Oddly, nowhere does it say: 'In 2003 Cheryl was named "Most Violent Thug" by a judge in a court case where she was accused of a racially motivated attack on a cleaner.'

* I would make a joke about this, but to be honest it'd be like shooting fish in a barrel.

** See above.

James Brown Has Powerful Testicles, Given to Him by the Government

Hurghhh. Hoowwwww. Hurgghhhowww. Get up. Like a sex machine. Etc.

Yes, what book would be complete without at least one reference to octogenarian fuck grunter James Brown?[1] Born in Barnwell, South Carolina, in 1933 and dying just in time for Christmas Day 2006, the mischievous, cheeky chap with the twinkle in his eye and the gun in his hand had been in prison and in police

---

[1]. Loads actually. Philip Pullman's *His Dark Materials* trilogy for a start. And anything by Clive Cussler. And *The Reader's Digest Driver's Atlas of Great Britain and Ireland.*

shootouts, was insane for most of the intervening years, and in 2002 was acquitted of charges of sexual harassment brought by a former employee.

Alas, James Brown didn't so much have a brush with the law as vigorously attack it with a Dyson pet hair vacuum cleaner.[2] In 1987 he was granted an audience with the pope,[3] who advised him to stick with music and not take up the ministry as he'd been considering at the time. Perhaps this snub from God's divine mouthpiece tipped him over the edge because soon after, at a meeting at his record company office, the Godfather of Soul produced a loaded shotgun and demanded that the assembled suits, lawyers, record company executives and insurance bigwigs tell him just exactly who had been using his personal toilet. This question, it would seem, was not on the meeting's agenda so instead of a discussion and, if you'll pardon the expression, any motions being carried, the boardroom gathering ended not with tea and biscuits but with a police

---

2. He served a sentence for larceny before he was 20, was generally arrested for domestic abuse and was charged with possession of PCP, assault and possession of illegal weapons. And in 1991 he had a set of new eyebrows tattooed onto his face. That in itself is not a crime, but it should be.

3. I think this was a Saturday evening ITV special. Bruce Forsyth's done it, Jimmy Tarbuck's done it. Even Joe Pasquale has done it. Popular with critics and with a celebrity audience including Simon Cowell, Ant and Dec, and Denise Van Outen, *An Audience with the Pope* was a great success but sadly didn't lead to the pope's own series.

chase during which 23 shots were fired at James Brown's erratically driven jeep, taking out both of his front tires. He was arrested high on PCP with his messy, sticking-up hair.

In 1991 he was paroled from prison. Four years later he had another international hit with 'Living in America' and then, just four years after that, the aforementioned testicle thing happened.

It was a sexual harassment case. A former assistant of Brown's, Lisa Agbalaya-Ross, took him to court in a $2 million lawsuit claiming that he sexually harassed her by 'grabbing her hips and making suggestive comments'. Brown's side argued that she had been made redundant when Brown's California office had been closed down and that she was simply 'a disgruntled former employee'. It was then that the alleged nature of James Brown's scrotal arrangement was brought into open court. At one point in the trial Ms. Ross, up on the stand and in front of the judge, counsel and jury, cryptically offered as evidence that 'Mr. James Brown has powerful testicles, given to him by the Government'. There followed a confused silence in court as this bizarre allegation echoed off the walls. And it was never ever explained.

James Brown was later cleared by a Los Angeles court of all allegations, testicular or otherwise. Perhaps the Brown balls weren't from the government after all. Perhaps they were a present from the pope.

Puff Party

For reasons known only to himself, fairly early on in his career the fur-covered, rapping Argos jewellery display case that is Sean Combs preferred to be known as 'Puff Daddy'. Oh I'm sure that's all very 'C' to the 'O' to 'O' to the 'L' in LA, where it's also equally 'rad' to shoot each other from cars, but I have to say, Sean, that over here in Britain it just made us snigger. You were called Puff Daddy. As though you were the daddy of the puffs. You were saying, through your name, that of all puffs, you were very much the daddy of them. You were then, in essence, telling us that you were a big batty homeboy.[1]

---

1. Which is, of course, politically correct reader, absolutely fine. I have no problem with homosexuals. I just wouldn't want to bum one.

Whether our stifled giggles made it across the Atlantic to your 'crib' or not I don't know but soon you decided to change your name. To P. Diddy. Oh dear, oh dear. That's no better, to be honest. That makes you sound like one of Ken Dodd's sidekicks[2] covered in piss. Thank God then that you're such an unassuming fellow; otherwise we might think you're a bit of a nob.

Oh hang on. I'd forgotten your 29th birthday.

Puff Daddy's 29th birthday was to be a party like no other. The Cristal was on ice, the bitches were hanging out and no doubt any rides had been well and truly pimped. But then when you've done all that, there's still the design of the invitations to be considered and brilliantly, and as only a hip hop king could demand of his local Prontaprint, these invitations not only *invited* the recipient to the 'do', but also reminded him or her just how lucky they were to have received such an invitation to such a party in the first place.

But that's not all. They also requested that each guest be 'overawed' at being able to attend a party that was 'part of history in the making', and then there was a list of instructions for each attendee. It ran thus:

---

2. Oh yes, who can forget Ken Dodd and his Diddymen? Well, if we try hard, we all can.

1. Ladies—waxing, pedicures and manicures are a must.[3]
2. Gents—no scuffed shoes or you're going to have a problem.[4]
3. All—outfits must be the flyest shot in your closet.[5]

Then there was an enclosed list of acceptable designers: Gucci (natch), Yves Saint Laurent, Versace and George Davies.[6] At the bottom, in gold lettering, was writ large the legend 'This will go down as the greatest party of all time'.

Really? Well, I don't remember it, do you? And I'm not sure exactly which part of 'history in the making' it was either. Presumably it was the part where everyone remembers a twat's party. Even though they don't. I bet they didn't even have Pass the Parcel[7] or jelly. Sorry, Mr. Diddy, but for me the only party that went down in

---

3. Waxing? Is he talking about the complete removal of a lady's front garden? Surely that's excessive as a dress code because at a party, ladies, assuming you're in your best frock, surely the mysteries of your downstairs area will remain a mystery? Oh no, hold on, I forgot: in P. Diddy Pufta's world, you're all hot 'be-aitches' and therefore will be in the nudey.

4. Not quite sure exactly *what* problem? Maybe something to do with dubbin?

5. Eh? The what?

6. Not really George Davies. Although to be fair, he is Asda's *premier* clothes designer. In fact, my friend and colleague Andy Hurst won't buy his shirts anywhere else. And they're only a few dollars each.

7. Joke about drugs removed for legal reasons.

history was one when I was about 15 and where I got off with Jenny White in Kevin Knight's bedroom while his parents were away. That and another school party where Louise Bazeley ran out of her bedroom (where she'd been getting off with Jason Aslett) in a topless panic because she thought her parents had come back early. Frankly, Mr. Diddy, your party doesn't even come close.

Not a Well(er) Man

Imagine getting an invitation that said this: 'Bonfire Night round at Noel and Liam's. Bring a bottle. And Paul Weller'. I may have paraphrased that but, invitation or no, so it was that one November the 5th, in the Gallaghers' back garden, a whole firework-code-following selection of pop stars found themselves sharing jacket potatoes, burnt sausages wrapped in tin foil and the small yet significant pleasure that is writing your name in the air with a sparkler.[1]

---

1. I hope they didn't invite Ben Volpeliere-Pierrot out of Curiosity Killed the Cat. There just wouldn't have been enough sparklers. Plus, he'd have

There's a huge bonfire,[2] fireworks aplenty and much wine flowing, mainly in the direction of Paul Weller, who has decided to really let his hair down and have some fun. Which is good because normally, in interviews and the like, he comes across as a right miserable cunt.[3] Noel is particularly pleased that Weller has turned up because he's one of his heroes and what better way to endear yourself to the great man than by letting him watch your dazzling display of rockets and silver fountains.[4] How can he fail to be impressed by a sausage and five things from a Black Cat firework selection box that have different names and packaging but, when lit, do exactly the same as each other? (In that they 'phut' out an equally unimpressive number of colored blobs before falling over and making a hole in the lawn.)

It was a tremendous evening. And as it wound down at around 1 a.m. the guests began to leave. But not

---

been late, what with not having a watch. (See 'Curiosity Time' in this book. Dunno whereabouts it is. You'll have to flick through.)

2. Possibly with all of Meg and Patsy's things on it.

3. No, really, he does. I once saw him at an awards ceremony and even his suit seemed bad-tempered.

4. Fireworks are named so as to conjure up the maximum possible amount of disappointment when you let them off. 'Krakatoa' is nothing of the sort, 'Cloudburst Air Strike' certainly wouldn't be anything for an Iraqi insurgent to lose sleep over and, when it ignites, even the amusingly named 'Golden Shower' is a bitter blow to all but the most forgiving pervert.

Weller. To Noel's delight the ex-Jam man and influence on a punk generation was more than happy to carry on drinking and even playing Noel's guitar. At around 3 a.m. though, Noel was ready to call it a night. He went to bed leaving Weller in the garden. Half an hour later he was awoken by something. He wasn't sure what. He lay there wondering what it might have been. And then he heard it again: the crackle of fire and the sound of rhythmic chanting. Like the man in the 'Night Before Christmas' poem before him, Noel was away to the shutters as quick as a flash. Below him, Paul Weller was still in the garden—but now Paul Weller had gone native. The Modfather was dancing around the rekindled fire, bare-chested with shirt waving wildly above his head, chanting 'Well-er! Well-er! Well-er!'[5] as if for all the world Golding's *Lord of the Flies* had been the story of marooned, demented pop stars in a garden on bonfire night instead of some filthy kids on an island blowing into a conch shell and killing each other.

Noel stood agape at the spectacle, gazing down from his bedroom window. In the light of a pale November moon his hero—composer and writer of 'Going Underground', 'Down in the Tube Station at Midnight', 'Stanley Road' and 'The Changingman'—was engaging in a ritualistic half-naked animal dance of fire in front

---

5. Well-er, well-er, well-er. As in his own name. Not as in 'Wella, wella, wella tell me more, tell me more' from *Grease*. I mean, that would be stupid.

of his very eyes. He threw open the window and responded to Weller's call of the wild:

'Go to bed, you silly old man,' he shouted.

Then he closed the window and went back to sleep.

It's the Wrong Dave Stewart, Gromit

A charming story, this. In fact the sort that sweet dreams are made of. On his way to Eurythmics main man and beardy miserabalist Dave Stewart's house,[1] scruffy voice-of-a-generation Bob Dylan knocked on what he thought was the right front door and asked if Dave Stewart lived there. Getting an answer in the affirmative from the lady of the house, Bob was informed that Dave had popped out and would be back soon.

---

1. Someone once told me that Dave Stewart has fiber-optic carpet. I don't know what this is, but I want some.

24

The great documentarian and reluctant figurehead of American unrest agreed to wait and was led into the lounge, where he sat on the sofa chatting to the lady and sipping a cup of tea. It is perhaps the cosiest, if most unlikely, scene in the history of rock.

It was shattered, however, when Dave Stewart arrived back an hour or so later. Largely because this was not the home of Dave Stewart the rock star but instead the home of Dave Stewart the plumber who lived in the next street. Needless to say Dave Stewart the plumber got the shock of his life when he found one of his musical heroes chatting to his old mum over a Garibaldi.[2]

Doubtless, from that moment on, Bob always had someone to call should his ball cock ever need a-changin'.[3]

---

2. The biscuit, obviously. Not the Italian revolutionary. And there is no actual evidence of a Garibaldi being involved. I made it up for 'color'.

3. Sorry.

Shit Hot

That well-worn trail of rock-'n'-roll-destroyed hotel rooms that meanders like a river of devastation across the globe is littered with the corpse bones of over-blown clichés like that one. Oh yes, when rock stars and accommodation collide, you can be sure there'll be mental happenings afoot: post-gig televisions out of windows, putting fish into groupies[1] and willingly eating Pringles with a 200% price mark-up from the minibar[2]—

---

1. See 'Stairway to Hell' in this very book.

2. It's outrageous. How dare they charge $5 for a few ovals of snack? Even something as simple as a small bag of nuts is about three quid in a minibar.

will these rock 'n' rollers stop at nothing in their quest for debauchery? But for sheer inventiveness and lasting effect none can beat Mike Patton, lead singer of Faith No More. That's because Mike Patton, lead singer of Faith No More, would take apart his hotel room's complimentary hair dryer, have a shit in it, and then screw it back together again.[3]

You've got to admire that. It's bad enough as it is, but let us together consider the inevitable, if you will, 'follow through' of such an act. One—he partakes of a Gentleman's Bathroom Adventure directly into an unscrewed hair dryer. Two—he reassembles it and (I hope) washes his hands.[4] Three—he checks out.

So in the words of Sue Barker on a particularly scatological edition of *A Question of Sport*, 'What

---

And don't get me started on the mixers. It's no wonder people drink the whiskey miniatures and piss in the bottles to fool housekeeping. And no wonder I've got up to five towelling robes that I've nicked. And 12 coathangers. And a TV. And three bathtaps. You have to take these things; it's the only language hotels understand.

3. Mr. Patton also once pissed all over Axl Rose's cue cards while Guns n' Roses were onstage and Axl was using them to shout his way through 'Sweet Child o' Mine'. He also had a shit in an orange juice carton, resealed it and put it back in Axl Rose's personal drinks vending machine. He doesn't seem to like Axl Rose much, does he? And this was even back in the days before fatty Axl looked an unholy cross between a *Stars in Their Eyes* Mick Hucknall and Predator like he does now.

4. Stands to reason. If you're going to be singing later you don't want to get shit on the mic.

happened next?' Well, oblivious to the Brown that's now nestling within the Braun, in comes the maid to clean the room. She vacuums, dusts, picks up something unidentifiable from the bed,[5] restocks the overly expensive Pringles, makes the bed, puts some more shampoo in the shower and leaves. At no point would she have any reason to pick up the hair dryer and give it a quick sniff. Job done.

Fast-forward to the next guest who is unfortunate enough to check into that room next morning. Maybe they're a fan of Faith No More, maybe they're not, but I'd argue that even a diehard FNM enthusiast would find it hard not to get worked up about what's about to happen. So they've checked in, unpacked and showered. Maybe they're enjoying a small $20 miniature of gin from the minibar. They're relaxed and happy. It's easy like Sunday morning. 'I may stroll down for lunch in half an hour,' they think. 'I must dry my hair.'

'Easy like Sunday Morning', a cover of the Commodores classic, was perhaps Faith No More's

---

5. Let's be honest. If Faith No More were happy to shit in a hairdryer then God only knows what could've been in the bed. In fact once, when asked where he got lyrical inspiration from, singer Mike Patton replied: 'My head, my ass, my toilet, my pillow, places like that.' These are not places one should examine too closely. Plus, any hotel cleaner worth their salt is always going to be wary of any band that have a song called 'Jizzlobber'.

biggest hit.[6] If, however, you're the unlucky guest in a Mike Patton–blessed hotel room you would do well to reflect on the irony, as *your* Sunday is going to be anything but easy. Largely because you've now got a hairful of finely sprayed boiling hot musician's shit.[7]

Quick, turn the page. This one feels dirty.

---

6. Reached number three in the UK charts, January 1993.

7. In Chile in 1995 he once invited the audience to spit in his open mouth. This man needs help.

Wet Wet Dry (Ice)

Richard Curtis. There he is, look, over there, putting the finishing touches to a lighthearted romantic comedy *and* making poverty history all in one go. I don't know how he does it, he's a mousy-haired philanthropic genius. But shortly before he cast Martine McCutcheon as tealady in one of the worst films ever made and long after he kindly waited until Ben Elton joined him on *Blackadder* before he made it funny, Richard Curtis penned the smash hit Britcom *Four Weddings and a Funeral*. Let's be honest, it was a good film.[1] Funny,

---

1. Well, good-ish.

touching and Hugh Grant stammering 'fuckitty fuck' a lot—what's not to like? Well, apart from Wet Wet Wet, obviously.

Wet × 3 had splashed onto the music scene in 1987 with that year's massive-selling *Popped In, Souled Out*,[2] and remarkably they were still big six years later when they were asked to cover the Troggs' 'Love Is All Around' for *Four Weddings*. But in the intervening gap they'd had another number one hit with a cover version of the Beatles classic 'With a Little Help from My Friends', and it was notable because it was an unlikely double A side with Billy Bragg.[3]

And it was in the charts for 11 weeks. And every week when the double-A-side single was featured on *Top of the Pops*, who do you think was invited on? Was it the four good-looking lads from Scotland and their charismatic[4] grinning[5] singer[6] or was it the dour, Essex curmudgeon with the out-of-tune guitar and strong political stance on the miners' strike? Correct. Ten points. And so it went on week after week until, a

---

2. Popped In, *Souled* Out. Do you see what they etc? Clever Wets.

3. Who was doing 'She's Leaving Home'. Both were on the album *Sergeant Pepper Knew My Father*, a cover of the whole Beatles album by 'Various Artists' all for Esther Rantzen's Childline charity in 1988.

4. And by 'charismatic' I mean smacked up on heroin.

5. And by 'grinning' I mean smacked up on heroin.

6. Ditto.

bit fed up that he had a number one single but wasn't allowed to go on TV to play it, Billy Bragg finally persuaded the *TOTP* producers to give him his moment of glory.

He told everyone—friends, family and dear old mum. His big moment had arrived. He was going on *Top of the Pops* to play his number one song. Billy was very, very excited right up until the moment when he realized that, because he'd never been allowed to do the song on TV, he didn't actually know the words very well. That was fine though, he'd write them down and tape them to the floor. So he did. And the rehearsal was fine. In fact, it was more than fine, it was a vintage Bragg performance. And then it was time for the recording.

'Now,' shouted the presenter,[7] 'this is his first *Top of the Pops* appearance so give it up for "She's Leaving Home"—it's Billy Bragg!' Cue muted applause from an audience of teenage girls who were disappointed it wasn't the Wets. Onstage, meanwhile, it was at this point that Bill noticed the blanket of dry ice that was now creeping across the stage. It hadn't been there during the rehearsal (dry ice is expensive) but it was now and it was completely obscuring the words that he didn't know. He muddled through the recording

---

7. This was 1988. Hmmm . . . Bruno Brookes or Janice Long, I reckon. Or maybe even Simon Mayo. Ah, those were the days.

half getting it right, half not, and looking like a rabbit not just caught in the headlights of a car, but a rabbit caught in the headlights of a car that's playing a song he doesn't know the words to on its stereo. At the end, because he'd looked a bit like a gaping fool, he asked the producers if they could do it again.

They said no. Billy's big moment was ruined. No wonder he's angry about stuff all the time.[8]

---

8. See 'Billy, Don't Be a Hero' somewhere in this book.

A Man Called Jim Webb

Who? Ah, well, follow me, young Padawan, for much to learn have you. You're right, Jim Webb is not a name with which you may be familiar. He's never been on heavy MTV rotation, has never been on *Top of the Pops* or *Later with Jools Holland* and has certainly never been famous at all, a bit like Pete Doherty shouldn't ever have been either. But Jim Webb certainly *deserves* to be famous because he's done some pleasingly mental things.

So who is he? Well, he's arguably one of the greatest songwriters that ever there was, having penned 'Galveston' and 'Wichita Lineman' for Glen Campbell, and 'MacArthur Park' for just about everybody. But I don't want to give you that. Oh no. I want to give you the story of the glider.

It's 1977 and Jim is working on a solo album with Beatles maestro George Martin and on said album, for some reason,[1] there's a song about gliding.[2] Wouldn't you know it but gliding is a passion of Jimmy Boy Webb and so he comes up with the elaborate and technically maniacal idea to mix actual glider noises into the song. Actual glider noises, mind you, not a sound effect. And so it was that he hired a 2,000-yard-long airstrip for the day and rigged it with stereo microphones every six feet. This required several tons of outside-recording equipment, including three trucks, 8,000 meters of cable, wind mufflers, a mobile studio and, let us not forget, a socking great glider.

Cometh the hour, Webb (who had decided to pilot the thing himself) climbed aboard his floaty death trap and took to the sky.[3] The mics were primed, the runway was clear, the tape was rolling. In a spot-on landing Webb whooshed onto the runway and

---

1. No one knows the reason. Drugs are odd things.

2. As in the 'sport' whereby you get in a wooden winged tube with no engine, get attached to a plane (with an engine), which then tows you into the sky and lets you go. If hunting is the sport of kings then gliding is the sport of mentals.

3. Behind a plane. A plane with an engine.

glid[4] down its entire length past every one of the few hundred stereo mics exactly as planned. The whole complex operation with its enormous budget and months of meticulous planning had been a complete success. Except that the completed effect sounds exactly like someone simply going 'ssssshhh'. That's it. That's all he got.

Ssssshhh, whisper it, but Jimmy Webb's a nutter.

---

4. Is 'glid' the past tense of 'glide'? I have no idea.

Holy Pigs

Pity the Church. As an institution it comes in for a fair amount of stick and in the last 25 years has seen its attendance figures—those all-important bums-on-pews—decline by 30%.[1] These days it seems that we're far more busy texting each other or happy slapping our PlayStations to have anything to do with all that God shit.[2]

---

1. Source: *The Christian Post*, August 2005. Article on church decline. That's right, I've just read an archive edition of *The Christian Post*. See the effort I've gone to to bring you the facts? And do you appreciate it? Do you, tits?

2. Coincidentally, also the title of Richard Dawkins's next book.

But churches need funds to repair their steeples and mount costly child abuse defense cases for their clergy and, let's be honest, there's only so many beetle drives and yard sales[3] that a church can have to try and keep poor Father O'Kiddietiddler out of the slammer, so alternative methods of fund-raising are sought and one church in London regularly rents out its holy space for the filming of rock videos.

Thus it was on one such occasion that Ozzy Osbourne found himself dressed in robes late at night perched high above the chapel floor on the carved, ornate altar while below him, squealing and mewling and running among the pews, were a thousand pigs. That's right, pigs. A thousand pigs all running about in what the director was doubtless hoping was a 'satanic' fashion.

Yes, rock and oinking roll, for such was to be the video for 'Miracle Man,'[4] the satirical tale of a hypocritical evangelistic hellfire preacher caught with his

---

3. Churches still do this. I was forced to go to these sorts of events as a child. A beetle drive is something to do with a church hall full of pensioners all drawing a beetle like a sort of mad game of insect bingo. I can't really remember. Actually reading that back it sounds mental. Perhaps I dreamt it. Hang on, I'll phone my mum. Wait there a sec . . . No. She confirms it. It did happen. She just tried to explain the rules to me but I put the phone down. If you're that interested, ask your nan or go to church.

4. From Ozzy's post-Sabbath solo album *No Rest for the Wicked*. Good, but for me not as tremendous as *Bark at the Moon*, where he ran around dressed as a Brummie werewolf.

pants down. Quite how this was to be communicated through the medium of porcine pew-running is anyone's guess but the designer had requested pigs and pigs he had got. But predictably it was the pigs that were the evening's undoing. The film crew had set up, the lights were lit, the pigs were in place and the Prince of Darkness was atop the altar, arms outstretched in crucifix pose, ready to mime to the song. The camera rolled to speed, the director called 'Action', the sound engineer pressed 'play' to bring in the track for Ozzy to sing along with and everyone held their breath. The first monster guitar chord obediently kicked in loud enough to wake the devil himself. And a thousand pigs simultaneously shat themselves all over the church.

The cleanup operation took a month.

The final word must, of course, go to Ozzy: 'I've been back there since, man, and it still fucking stinks of shit.'

Heaven Is a Place on Eargghhth

She was lead singer of the GoGos and already the subject of a much-rumored but little- (actually, to be honest, *never*) seen dressing room home movie of her 'entertaining' herself just before a gig in New York,[1] but

---

1. Apparently. I've had a quick look on the internet but to no avail. Well, there was some avail but a) it wanted my credit card details and, b) I'm not sure it was actually Belinda Carlisle. I did, during my research, find a similar home video purporting to be the blond one out of Hear'Say diddling herself in a public toilet. On reflection, I'm not sure that was 100% genuine either. Perhaps if the blond one out of Hear'Say is reading this and *has* ever diddled with her own mimsy in a public bog while being filmed she could drop me a line and let me know. Similarly Ms. Carlisle.

it was in the late 80s at the height of her solo success that Belinda Carlisle nearly killed a man.

It was in London and her record company had fixed up a number of European press interviews. One journalist who was ushered through the door for his five or ten minutes with the pop goddess was a German hack who suffered from a pronounced stammer. He was also very, very nervous, confronted as he was with his very own piece of Belinda Carlisle-shaped Heaven on Earth.[2]

As he sat down to ask Belinda his first question[3] his nervousness, coupled with his speech impediment, meant that—instead of words—what came out of his mouth was a quick succession of jerky sounds which, as he struggled to make himself heard, only got worse as he became locked in an endless spiral of bulging eyes, sweaty discomfort and vocal frustration.

To her eternal credit, Belinda jumped immediately to a totally wrong conclusion. Assuming the sputtering German gentleman was epileptic and choking on his tongue she wrestled the man to the floor as she yelled for help. Thus it was that our stuttering friend found himself pinned to the ground by Belinda and her six-

---

2. 'Heaven Is a Place on Earth' was of course her debut solo single. And yes, I *have* crowbarred it in.

3. The records do not state what it was. 'Can I see your home movie?' perhaps?

foot-tall manager, the latter sticking a meaty fist down the back of the poor man's throat and attempting to pull his tongue out through his teeth and hold it there.

The interview was cancelled.

Hey, You, Get off of My Pie

It's Toronto in 1994 and someone has just eaten Keith Richards's shepherd's pie. And he's gone absolutely mental.[1] Yes, the Stones are on tour (when aren't they?) and this time it's the one about doing voodoo in someone's lounge.[2] It's, oh, almost 20 minutes to showtime and time for Keith's tea. Tonight it's yummy shepherd's pie and he's been looking forward to it all day.[3] But wait

---

1. More mental. He's already mental, obviously.

2. Or whatever.

3. And who wouldn't after a hectic day slaving over a hot teaspoon?

a minute, what's this? Where has it gone? The pie was here, but now it's missing. Who's been eating Keith's pie? Who has been in here while Keith's been out and eaten his lovely pie? How dare they? Yes, just like those three bears caught up in a not too dissimilar tale, when Keith found that some Goldilocks-like figure had been to his dressing room and eaten his beloved pie all up,[4] he roared his disapproval. That was it. The limit had been reached and he promptly sat down in a huff and refused to go onstage.

Hurried talks were had, hapless minions were dispatched back and forth and management were called in as the allotted time for the gig to begin came and went. Still Keith wouldn't budge and still no one had owned up to the mystery of the missing pie. Eventually a compromise was reached. Keith would go onstage, but only if somebody brought him another pie. More hurried talks were had and this time minions were dispatched to find chefs. The concert should have started 20 minutes ago so the chefs set about making a new pie. And Keith had dictated that it couldn't be any old pie either. It had to be another shepherd's pie and not just any old shepherd's pie but a shepherd's pie to match the high standards Keith insists upon when it comes to ground beef with a seasoned mashed potato topping.

---

4. There is no record of that person also having broken his wooden chair or having slept in his tiny bed.

45

Eventually, the replacement pie was brought to Keith by no fewer than six people. He ate one mouthful, then picked up his guitar and headed to the stage, where the rest of the band were glaring at him waiting to go on. As one crew member recalls: 'I think he just did it to annoy Mick.'[5]

---

5. To be fair, it was probably Mick who ate the shepherd's pie in the first place, just to annoy Keith.

I Warn You, This Is Quite Unpleasant[1]

Here's a game of six degrees of separation. Can you get from legendary record producer Trevor Horn to a cocktail of Kurt Cobain's snot and piss (and worse) in less than six moves? No? Don't tire yourself, allow me.

Cast your mind back to the birth of MTV. Or, if you weren't born then, don't. It was August 1, 1981, and Music Television announced its arrival with, appropriately enough, the video for 'Video Killed the Radio Star' by The Buggles, and The Buggles was an appalling name for an appalling idea for a band fronted by Trevor

---

1. Seriously, it is. If you don't like unpleasant, look away now.

Horn.[2] So there's the Trevor Horn connection and it gets you from Trevor Horn to MTV. Skip through the intervening years and you arrive at the 1992 MTV Music Awards, which boasted, among a stunning line-up, Nirvana, Guns n' Roses, Metallica, Def Leppard and erm, Elton John. Ah, see, now we're getting closer. Thing was, also present was Courtney Love, Kurt Cobain's mentally ill then-girlfriend, and as such she began berating Guns n' Roses' Axl Rose about how he'd 'sold out' and become 'a pantomime dame like Elton John' and how Nirvana would 'kick their ass'. Axl, a man also not known for his reticence, came back with the terribly Wildeian response of 'Shut the fuck up, bitch' and thus much rock star glowering commenced across the wilds of the backstage catering area.

Meanwhile, Axl's awesome rock ballad 'November Rain' had been the most requested video on MTV that year and the plan was for him to perform it live on a grand piano that would rise up through the stage as a fitting climax to the show. Obviously then, following the earlier exchange of pleasantries, a riled up[3] Courtney

---

2. Trevor Horn was almost single-handedly responsible for Frankie Goes to Hollywood and the Art of Noise, formed ZTT Records, and worked with the Pet Shop Boys, Seal, ABC and Dollar. He is also to blame for the proliferation throughout the world of those big 80s glasses that look stupid when worn on the face. See also Christopher Biggins, Timmy Mallett, Su Pollard and Bono.

3. And by riled up I mean drug-stuffed.

and Kurt couldn't let this moment pass without sabotage and so crept beneath the stage with the notion that they would 'deposit' various bodily fluids onto the piano keyboard. Earlier, just over there (←) in fact, I said it was a cocktail of snot and piss. And so it was, but I spared you the rest of it until you got down here. I'm afraid there were other, even more distasteful ingredients to that cocktail than simple snot and piss. I'm sorry if you're eating as you read this or on a train surrounded by people or something but I'm afraid to report there was also erm, well, jizz. Spunk, if you will.[4] Sperm. Spermatozoa. I know, I know, but don't shoot the messenger.[5] Oh yes, and there was some spit as well. Anyway, this ungodly mixture was 'slimed'[6] across the keys of Axl's grand piano and left there by a giggling Kurt and Courtney, amused no doubt at the thought of Axl rising stagewards, hammering out the opening chords to his love song on a piano keyboard laced with pools of gruesome nasty.[7]

Thing was, unbeknownst to them, Axl wasn't going to be playing the piano that night. Scheduled to play as a special treat for fans was instead none other than

---

4. This is not an instruction. At least, not if you're on a train.

5. Or indeed over him.

6. And I use that in the *Ghostbusters* sense of the word.

7. Kind of puts McCartney and Wonder's 'Ebony and Ivory' into perspective, doesn't it?

Elton John. And thus it was that on this occasion 'November Rain' became November something-else-entirely.

It's not often you feel sorry for Elton John, is it?

Manic Street Preachers

Long before they issued us with the warning that if we tolerated this, then our children would be next,[1] the Manic Street Preachers was home to an eccentric gentleman by the name of Richey Edwards, who has since become the subject of one of rock 'n' roll's biggest mysteries, simply by disappearing.[2] Richey

---

1. A handy tip from the Manics there for testing your infant's bathwater with your elbow.

2. Just ahead of their US tour to promote *The Holy Bible* album, Richey walked out of the Embassy Hotel in London. Fifteen days later his car was found near 'a notorious suicide spot' near the Severn Bridge in Bristol.

Edwards vanished in 1995 and has never been seen since,[3] but we are concerned here with a time when he could very much still be seen, specifically by himself, in a mirror.

In 1988 the Manics[4] are doing an interview with a well-known music mag, and for the accompanying photo shoot Richey has decided, as it's the height of the AIDS scare,[5] to get a razor blade and carve the letters 'HIV' into his chest so that it would become a bloody message of awareness for 'the kids'. This is obviously both cool *and* hip so, blade in hand, the mad Manic disappears into the dressing room[6] and emerges ten

---

3. Although various sightings have been claimed. A couple of years ago, for instance, a fan swore blind he'd seen Richey in a tea shop in Australia. Before that he'd been seen staring out to sea from a Tenerife clifftop. Last year he was sighted on the surface of Elvis. Actually, when The Darkness recruited a new bass player called *Ritchie* Edwards in 2005, fan speculation went into overdrive that it was the missing musician. It wasn't.

4. Richey had just joined. His main contribution was to write some songs, mime the guitar and self-harm his limbs.

5. It's the year of the government putting leaflets through our letterboxes warning us not to die of ignorance (or, presumably, AIDS), and former *Late Late Breakfast Show* outside broadcast patsy Mike Smith appeared on BBC1 at 7 p.m. showing viewers how to put a condom on correctly. Not on himself, I hasten to add. It was onto a dildo. Still, it was groundbreaking stuff.*

6. Just the dressing room. Don't panic. Everyone knew where he was.

* This did happen, didn't it? I didn't dream this, did I? Oh God. No, I'm sure it did. It was a serious BBC sex education drive at a time when everyone was scared of getting The AIDS. Wasn't it? Anyone? Poor Mike Smith. That whole Michael Lush thing wasn't his fault.

minutes later, bare-chested and gory with the letters boldly, and I imagine painfully, cut into his torso. Problem is, he's done it in the mirror so guess what? Yes. You're quite right. They're backwards. Richey Manic is now a walking, bleeding advertisement for 'VIH' which I think is the accepted abbreviation for the Vancouver Island Helicopter service.[7]

The Manic Street Preachers still appeared in the magazine that month in photo form but the picture was reversed. Thus the message of the dangers of The AIDS was quite firmly communicated to 'the kids' but, unfortunately, the other message—that Richey Edwards was a twat—has sadly been lost for ever.[8]

---

7. Genuinely, it is. I've checked. Actually, by a magnificent stroke of luck, it's also the abbreviation for Virus d'Immuno-Deficience Humaine, which is French for HIV. Is he clever or stupid? You decide. (Answer: stupid.)

8. Note to crazy Manics fans: please don't write in and complain that I called him a twat, but if you must, at least try to do it the right way round.

The Baker Street Irregularity

Altogether now—ner ner ner ner ner ner ner neeeeer, ner ner ner ner ner ner ner neeeeeer, ner ner ner ner ner ner ner ner ner ner neeeeerrrrr—ner ner ner ner. Of course, that's instantly recognizable[1] as the theme tune to hit 80s and possibly early 90s daytime quiz show *Blockbusters*, hosted by Bob Holness. What an excellent program it was too. It was a deft battle of wits with, inexplicably, one contestant against two as they battled to get from one side of the Blockbusters board to the other in

---

1. Although not when written down.

order to be in with a chance of playing on the Gold Run.[2]

But aside from being the genial host of everyone's favorite quiz ever, Bob Holness, it came to light, had also been the sax player for the solo on Gerry Rafferty's 'Baker Street'. Yes, it seemed that the huge hit of 1978 by the ex-Stealer's Wheeler and pal of Billy Connolly[3] featured none other than Holness on sax. Wow. That is hella cool.

In fact, go and listen to it now. If you don't have it, download it off iTunes immediately as it's a cracking track. Listen . . . listen . . . yep . . . listen carefully because here comes the sax bit. Listen to that. Sweeping, isn't it? Majestic. Haunting. Epic, you might say. Hard to imagine, isn't it, that it's being blown by the amiable host of *Take a Letter* and Yorkshire TV's *Raise the Roof*?[4]

---

2. Or something. I seem to remember there were letters and they made a path across the board somehow. Bob would ask questions like 'What B did the Sex Pistols never mind?' And then someone would ask for 'a P, please, Bob' and then everyone sniggered. And those were, in essence, the rules of *Blockbusters*.

3. Indeed, Rafferty also wrote 'Stuck in the Middle with You' as heard on the *Reservoir Dogs* soundtrack and with the Big Yin was in a folk trio called the Humblebums in the late 60s. See, I can be informative as well as sweary and sarcastic.

4. He was also a Radio 1 DJ. One of the first alongside Terry Wogan, Jimmy Young and Kenny Everett. And now we've got Chris Moyles. Can't life be cruel?

Yes, it is hard to imagine. Because it isn't. It was non-sense. It was a joyous story first put about by writer and broadcaster Stuart Maconie when he worked for the *NME*.[5] Holness, to his eternal credit, went along with the story and later also claimed he'd played the main guitar part on Derek and the Dominoes' 'Layla' and was the mysterious figure that caused Elvis to crack up during that 'laughing version' of 'Are You Lonesome Tonight?' Meanwhile Maconie got bored and started a new rumor that David Bowie owned all the rights to Connect 4.[6]

What larks.

---

5. The actual player was session musician Raphael Ravenscroft, who, weirdly, was an early James Bond, appearing as the spy in a 1956 South Africa, radio version of *Moonraker*. No, really. Would I lie to you like Maconie? Would I?

6. Popular children's game. Like Buckaroo but with less donkey.

Boys Who Like Girls

It was a time when Britpop ruled the waves; Oasis were king, Jarvis Cocker was a god and someone, some-where, had actually bought a record by Menswear.[1] I know, hard to believe, isn't it? It was 1995 and out of the ashes of Colchester[2] came a band called Blur.

The Essex three- (and later four-) piece had just hit the big time with their song 'Girls and Boys', a song about girls and boys, and lead singer Damon Albarn was living with his then girlfriend, Justine Frischmann.

---

1. For more Menswear anecdotage, see 'A Fine Time' within this tome.

2. A metaphor. It hadn't actually burned down or anything. Not since the Romans anyway. Although some argue that the Mersea Road area of Colchester could do with a razing.

Eagle-eyed readers[3] will doubtless swoop on the name, saying: 'Hang on—Justine Frischmann? But isn't she the lead singer of . . . Oh hang on. I know this. She's the lead singer of . . . er . . . oh bloody hell. I know this. Don't tell me. I'll get it. She's the singer with . . . no, it's gone. Go on, tell me.'[4]

At this point in time though, Justine isn't famous and thus as Blur hit the charts for the first time Damon can only surmise that the growing army of fans now gathering outside his house each night are Blur obsessives, waiting to catch a glimpse of their hero. Every evening, as the band's fortunes gather pace and the group gets bigger and bigger, every evening from about ten o'clock to midnight there they are, gathering outside like unseasonal carol singers in anoraks and Blur beanie hats. Such, assumes Damon, is the price of fame.

One night, as he arrives home late, he sees the large group keeping vigil as usual in the road outside his house and notices, perhaps for the first time, that they are mostly all blokes. Surreptitiously, his own hat[5]

---

3. Or eagle-fingered, if you're reading the braille version.

4. Elastica.

5. We don't know what sort. Possibly it wasn't a Blur one. It definitely wouldn't have been an Oasis one.*

* Oasis and Blur didn't get on. They were like protons and neutrons in a nucleus. Except that protons in a nucleus didn't go round saying they wished that the neutrons in the same nucleus would die of The AIDS.

59

drawn deep down over his ears and collar up, he joins the group staring at his house and asks what the craic[6] is.

'This is that bloke from Blur's gaff, is it?' he says to one house-gawking fan.

'What?' comes the reply. 'Dunno, mate.'

Suddenly puzzled, our Damon looks toward his house, where there's a light on in the upstairs window.

'We come down 'cos the bird that lives here has absolutely no idea the curtains are see-through and she gets undressed in front of the window every night,' confides the lad. 'She's got no idea we can see her but if you hang round a bit you'll see the lot. Muff and everything. Every night she does it. Word's got round so every night we come and watch.'

There is a pause before he continues: 'So who's this Blur bloke you're on about then?'

Boys. They love a bit of it.[7]

---

6. He wasn't Irish, so he may not have actually said exactly this. But it doesn't matter. I think the Irish and their made-up words are charming.

7. 'Parklife'!

The Adventures of
Brinsley Schwarz

Brinsley Schwarz[1] were a bunch of 70s pub rockers whose publicity company decided on the mother of all publicity stunts. They would charter a jet to fly dozens of UK journalists to New York to watch them play live[2] and thus, having bribed the hacks with free flights and as much insipid airplane beer as they could handle, they would thereby ensure favorable reviews for the group and thus increase those all-important album sales back home.

---

1. Named after the band's guitarist, Brinsley Schwarz. Oh dear, oh dear, oh dear.

2. At the legendary Fillmore East Auditorium. It was April 3, 1970, fact fans.

So far, so expense account. However, it was then that things began to go completely Tim Westwood.[3] First, the journo-jet developed problems somewhere over the Atlantic and had to turn round and land at Ireland's Shannon Airport, where it promptly stayed for 24 hours. The disgruntled ladies and gentlemen of the press were immediately given access to a free bar. Meanwhile, 3,000 miles away on the Canadian border, two of the band were refused entry into the US due to an old drugs bust.[4] Then the journalists that *did* manage to show up for the gig got so drunk waiting for it to start that they couldn't even see, let alone review, anything. And then the sticky carpets and foamy real ale behemoth that was The Schwarz discovered that they had to pay for the whole lot out of their record company advance.[5] This would have been fine had

3. Tim Westwood. DJ. Even worse than Pete Tong. Thus the name 'Tim Westwood' should be invoked as slang when something goes very, very, very Pete Tong indeed.

4. Americans frown on you entering their country if you've ever taken drugs. It's sticking to strict rules like this that makes them such a well-adjusted nation.

5. Scientifically this is now known as the Bros Effect. The mathematical equation for the Bros Effect goes like this: talent less than hype equals money plus more money than you can handle divided by amount of over-hype disproportionate to talent equals advance pissed up a wall plus amount owed to record company equals nothing.*

* Written by mathematicians as $tl < hy = \$\$ + \$\$\$\$ \div \$\sqrt{hy} \neq tl = \text{🏃} + (-)\$\$\$\$\$ = 0$

those all-important record sales ever occurred but sadly, even though they headlined the first Glastonbury Festival, supported Wings and appeared in *Stardust* with David Essex,[6] all five consequent Brinsley Schwarz albums systematically failed to grace the charts in much the same way that Gary Glitter will never again be gracing the repair department of PC World. Then they split up.

In the ensuing years Schwarz bassist Nick Lowe went on to become Nick Lowe, and none other than Elvis Costello covered their '(What's So Funny 'bout) Peace, Love and Understanding', but this didn't stop the by now defunct Brinsley Schwarz *still* owing their record company $60,000 for their one New York appearance over 30 years ago. The debt was finally cleared in 2005, when the actor Bill Murray sang 'Peace, Love and Understanding' in the movie *Lost in Translation*. It was then that Schwarz drummer Billy Rankin finally got a taste of the big time: a royalty check for $1,000.[7]

---

6. Or perhaps, because of this.

7. As a footnote, nearly even a proper one this time, I am indebted to Penguin employee Dave Atkinson, who tells me that the story has an even happier ending than the one described above. Dave correctly points out that '(What's So Funny 'bout) Peace, Love and Understanding' was also covered by Curtis Stigers on the soundtrack to the shit Whitney Houston/Kevin Costner film *The Bodyguard*. The album went 17 times platinum, thanks in the main to a pre-crack Whitney shouting 'I-I-I-I Will

Always Love Youuuuuu' into Costner's startled face. Nick Lowe (who wrote 'What's So Funny . . .') was thus 'suddenly presented with a royalty cheque of around a million quid followed fairly shortly by another one—just about enough in fact to buy his own recording studio in Islington'. Thanks, Dave. Although, while it may be a happy ending for Nick Lowe, the fact remains that the drummer still only got a few hundred quid. Just about enough in fact to buy, say, a new Hoover in Curry's Digital.

The Bones Is Mine

In a darkened tent somewhere in the grounds of a circus sideshow marked 'freakish', the lone, sorry figure of something that could once have been human steps nervously into the light. The assembled onlookers gasp as they catch sight of a grotesquely disfigured face, half hidden in waxy shadow. 'I am not an animal. I am a human being!' it bellows. 'And by the way, I never touched those kids.'

That's right, I led you up the garden path of the Elephant Man, John Merrick,[1] but then rudely shoved

---

1. He was immortalized as 'John' in the 1980 David Lynch film but in fact his real name was Joseph. Although I imagine his mates called him Mongface.

you through the front door of Michael Jackson.[2] But not without purpose, for the tragic stories of these two fairground unattractions are inextricably linked in ways that don't simply involve sharing unusually rare nose shapes and a head that should be in a bag. And that is because in 1987 Jacko tried to buy John Merrick's bones.

What he planned to do with them is anyone's guess[3] but he apparently offered $50,000[4] for them crazy elephant bones.[5] Sadly he was shit out of luck because all of Mr. Merrick's remains[6] had been destroyed in an air raid on the London Hospital in the Second World War. All that was left circa 1987, and indeed now, were plaster casts of his head, arm and foot.[7]

And so we shall never know Jacko's big plans for the moldering Merrick. The King of Pop has of course long had a very public obsession with his own appearance, so perhaps he was simply going to put the skeleton on display in his gaudy, gingerbread house. Perhaps

---

2. Not somewhere you'd want to go. Ever.

3. Here's mine: he was going to make soup. Deformed soup.

4. At current exchange rates, that's about a pound.

5. An inspired line, credit for which belongs to the Barenaked Ladies and their excellent song 'If I Had $1000000'.

6. His organs were kept in jars. Like jam. Deformed jam.

7. Which were borrowed by Madame Tussauds in 2005, when they were modeling Wayne Rooney. Fact.

he thought he'd found a kindred spirit in the lumpy, misshapen, waxy monster that was both a fascinating medical conundrum and the stuff of a child's nightmare.

Can't imagine why.

Who's Gonna Drive You Home . . . ?[1]

A good question, to which the answer would be, if you're a rock star, your chauffeur is. But how can he drive you home, Mr. Keith Moon, if you've just killed him with your Bentley?

Yes, the erstwhile drummer from The Who, who,

---

1. This is of course a line from the Cars' classic 'Drive', first released in 1984, when it got to number five in the UK chart. It was re-released in summer 1985 after it was used to accompany harrowing images of fly-faced African children during Live Aid. This time it got one place higher to number four. It was kept off the top spot by 'Dancing in the Street', which was used to accompany harrowing images of David Bowie and Mick Jagger prancing about like a couple of wrinkled nob-ends.

let's face it, was no stranger to the way of the hedonist, famously also owned a Rolls-Royce, a car which came to prominence when he drove it into a hotel swimming pool,[2] but he also had a Bentley and it's that car that concerns us here. Well, specifically his Bentley and the small Hertfordshire market town of Hatfield. Dating back to Saxon times, the village of Hatfield was first known as 'Hetfelle' and then became known as 'Haethfeld' when, around 970, King Edgar gave 5,000 acres of land to the monastery of Ely. Records pick up again in the year 1226, when Henry III granted the Bishops of Ely rights to an annual four-day fair and a weekly market.[3] And since then, nothing much has happened in, around, to or for Hatfield. Apart from one night in 1970 when The Who rolled into town.

They were there for a gig. At Hatfield's main disco, referred to colloquially by locals as 'Hatfield's main disco', there was to be much windmilling of arms and plenty of pinballing wizardry. Unfortunately, though, the prospect of The Who showing up at *all* had much irked the local skinhead population, who decided to

---

2. It is disputed whether this act actually ever really took place. Moon's biographer, Tony Fletcher, denies it happened but none other than Roger Daltrey claims to have seen the bill.

3. Source: Hatfield town council's website. I can also report directly from this valuable resource that the council's recent draft budget was approved and that the members of the Leisure Committee recommended that there be no amendments to the proposed fees and charges.

show their disapproval of the music[4] by hanging around outside the venue spitting and looking aggressive. The gig itself passed without incident[5] but afterward, as the band went their separate ways, Keith Moon walked out into the cold night air to meet his driver, who'd brought the Bentley round to the stage door to pick him up. It was at this point that they were surrounded by the less-than-friendly skinheads. A nervous Moon clambered into the back while the driver tried to drive through the throng but the problem was that they weren't really moving out of the way. In an act of admirable yet ultimately foolish bravery, the driver got out to clear a path. It was at this point that Keith, sitting in the back, panicked. He jumped into the driver's seat, knocked the car into gear and lurched forward. Big mistake. The car ran over the chauffeur and killed him. And the skinheads ran away. Still, at least Hatfield's now known for something. They should put up a plaque or something.[6]

*

4. Skinheads weren't big fans of The Who. It was the 70s and they just liked Skrewdriver* and punching people in the face.

5. Obviously there was the usual smashing up the equipment stuff but, you know, frankly that's old hat (field).

6. Go to the council's website and email them about it. Perhaps some of their leisure funding could be diverted toward an 'It was on this spot in 1970 that Keith Moon ironically ran over his driver' commemorative bench or something.

* BBC Radio 2 presenter Mark Radcliffe was once the drummer in Skrewdriver. But before they were racist.

Postscript: Actually, I've just remembered that Hatfield is also where the custard stops,[7] so that's two things it's known for. Dead chauffeurs and custard.[8]

---

7. According to Kenny Everett, that is. I'm not explaining it. Read his book *The Custard Stops at Hatfield.* Oh, you can't. It's criminally out of print.

8. Rejected original lyric from 'Food, Glorious Food' in Lionel Bart's *Oliver!*

Pink Sabbath

It's the 70s and, apart from Marston's Bitter Party 7s,[1] pub bombs and a comedy accent, Black Sabbath are perhaps Birmingham's most famous export. Tales of their debauched approach to life on the road are the stuff and nonsense of legend, but long before the days

---

1. These were sort of a seven-pint tin of warm beer traditionally served at parties and joked about on TV by Jasper Carrott. As a child I used to watch, fascinated, as my Dad would bring one out every Christmas and set about jabbing two holes in the top ('one for the beer to come out and one to let air in') with the sharp bit of a tin opener. Ingeniously, for a big tin of beer, the tin was exactly the wrong shape and size to successfully get any beer out of.

when he was simply a bumbling figure of fun with a terrifying, shouty wife, lead singer Ozzy Osbourne was quite simply *the* bat-snacking[2] King of British Heavy Metal. With a terrifying, shouty wife.

According to the popular moral belief of mental people and/or Christians at the time, Black Sabbath were also Satanists who regularly worshipped the dark Lord Mephistopheles[3] both on- and backstage. Of course, the band denied this,[4] but in rock 'n' roll a reputation is a reputation[5] and thus it was that back in those dark, satanic days, a noted female journalist from a noted music magazine had to go on tour with Black Sabbath and, due to their unhallowed and hellish

---

2. Don't do it, kids. Don't eat bats. You might get rabies. Dairylea Lunchables are best avoided for the same reason.

3. Aka Satan aka Beelzebub aka The Dark One aka Jasper Carrott arriving at your party clutching seven pints of tinned Skol.

4. The moral majority were somewhat vindicated when 30 years later, the Devil came to punish and torture the eternally damned Ozzy by returning to Earth and taking the form of a particularly frisky quad bike.

5. Just ask Patsy Kensit.

APOLOGY

In footnote 2, above, I may have accidentally implied that it is possible to contract the disease rabies from a well-known cheese and breadstick dip-based snack. I would like to apologize unreservedly for this remark and would point out that at no time has anyone contracted any form of brain disease from this product, nor are they ever likely to, even if they eat 50 of them in one go. I am happy to set the record straight.

standing throughout polite society, was more than a little worried about it.

However, she needn't have panicked. When she got on the tour bus she discovered that the arch devil worshippers had replaced the curtains in her bunk with pink frilly ones just to make her feel at home.

Bless them.

Lost in Transfusion

Early in the morning, when he wakes up, portly and definitely-not-gay karaoke rehab gurner Robbie Williams looks, by his own admission, like KISS but without the makeup. This, despite the fact that he's probably too young to remember exactly who KISS were.

In 1977 the leather-haired cartoon rock band of which Robbie spake were all metal codpieces, armor plating, big platform boots and demonic face paint,[1]

---

1. They looked as if a suicide bomber had stood next to them and detonated a dressing-up box full of Lycra and melted wax crayons.

apart, that is, from drummer Peter Criss, who would inexplicably dress as a cat. As they'd based this look on that of any number of comic book superheroes (with the possible exception of the cat) it was only a matter of time before they were immortalized in their *own* comic.

But this was to be no *Beano*. When the plans for the KISS comic were literally on the drawing board it soon became very clear that the catapult and gobstopper world of the likes of *Whizzer and Chips* was a very long way away. And that was because the KISS comic was drawn in the band's own blood.

Presumably on the theory that no one had ever caught hepatitis from a pamphlet,[2] the band happily agreed that their red-raw rock plasma should be mixed with the printer's ink for the first edition of the publication with the does-exactly-what-it-says-on-the-tin title of *KISS: The Comic*. And so it came to pass that the medically inadvisable-to-read magazine was eventually published to no great acclaim, as was this certificate by a Notary Public, duly called in to authorize the process:

This is to certify that KISS members, Gene Simmons, Ace Frehley, Paul Stanley and Peter Criss, who is the one dressed as a cat,[3] have each donated blood which is being

---

2. At time of writing. At time of reading, however, thousands may have died from a deadly pandemic of Book Flu.

3. Author's own parenthesis.

collectively mixed with the red ink to be used for the first issue of the Marvel/KISS comics. The blood was extracted on February 21st, 1977 at Nassau Coliseum and has been under guarded refrigeration until this day when it was delivered to the Borden Ink plant in Depew, New York.

My favorite bit is the bit that says 'under guarded refrigeration'. If I were KISS, that's what I'd have called my next album.

Mercury Rising

It's a well-known fact that, according to horizontal-toothed vest wearer Freddie Mercury, fat-bottomed girls make the world go round. A good singer-song-writer he may have been, but I'm afraid he was useless when it came to understanding the laws of Newtonian gravitational physics. In fact he was far more interested in dwarfs.[1]

---

1. It's not what you're thinking. There is no suggestion he had bottom sex with any of them. Read on.*

* Actually a girl I know once did have sex with a dwarf. She said that, during foreplay, he used his whole arm. I know, I know. I'm just telling you what she told me. Again, don't shoot the messenger.

Allow me to elaborate. Not just dwarfs per se, but dwarfs[2] carrying huge silver platters of cocaine above their tiny heads. Allow me to elaborate again. Not just dwarfs carrying huge silver platters of cocaine above their tiny heads, but dwarfs carrying huge silver platters of cocaine above their tiny heads at parties.

Parties. Oh yes. And Queen's were legendary. Let's face it, Freddie Mercury was flamboyant enough as it was with his yellow jacket, his Village People–style facial hair and his protruding teeth, so just imagine the sort of party he'd throw. Decadent is not the word. Actually, decadent is exactly the word. Naked people, booze, dancers . . . naked people covered in booze and dancers—if you didn't clamor for a ticket to this sort of party you were either unfashionably boring or Roger Taylor. But let's be honest, lots of showbiz parties have naked people, booze and dancers. Some even have a dead bloke in a pool with a broken vodka bottle up his arse[3] but only Freddie Mercury's had dwarfs bringing round platters of cocaine. And what's more, these dwarfs would be in costume. I don't mean from a panto either. There'd be no comedic pointy boots and hats and diamond mine pickaxes on display here. Oh no.

---

2. Is it 'dwarfs' or 'dwarves'? I'm not sure. I think both could be right. It's like 'hoofs' and 'hooves', isn't it? Or 'poofs' and 'pooves'. No offense, Freddie.

3. Don't they, Mr. Barrymore?

That would be stupid. These were barechested dwarfs in leather chaps and studded collars; this was the sort of costume that would give Snow White a heart attack.[4] But there's a logic to it all if you think about it. If cocaine is to be offered to guests at your party what better way than to have it served on top of a dwarf? It's going to be at the right height for a small bend and a sniff, isn't it? There'd be no getting on your knees next to the coffee table, oh no. This way the coke comes to you and it's easily within reach. Mr. Mercury had thought this through. The man was a genius.

But is it true? Well, you may have heard the rumors and counter-rumors over the years but all I can offer by way of any evidence whatsoever is that some years ago a roadie lifted the lid of a flightcase[5] backstage and showed me a photo that was stuck there on the inside. It was of a dwarf, attired as described, holding aloft a silver serving tray of suspicious-looking white powder.[6] In the background, slightly fuzzy and out of focus, was a man who looked very much to me like the late

---

4. A tactic the Wicked Queen never considered. Would have saved her a fortune in poisoned apples.

5. Big box for the storing of stage concert equipment. I've mostly put this footnote in for the benefit of my mum, who may not know what one is. Oh, and Mum, if you are reading this, don't read the bit about the dwarf having arm-sex with a girl.

6. I suppose it could have been talc. After all, all that leather must chafe a dwarf.

Freddie Mercury.[7] The roadie had previously been on tour with Queen and even claimed to have been to such parties. After Freddie died and Queen stopped touring, he'd bought a bunch of flightcases from the band and had found the photo inside. He told me never ever to tell anyone.

Oops.

---

7. Admittedly it could have also been Lord Lucan or a horse wearing a joke moustache.

Oh What a Feeling, When You're Stuck up in the Ceiling

Quick, everyone, put down your Panda Pops lemonade and start dancing because it's the song that goes 'Ba ba ba ba baaa ba ba ba ba baaaaaaaa'[1] ★*flings self around so hard at school disco that buckle flies up off pointy suede shoe and hits eye.[2]*★

Yes, it's 1978, the Teardrop has exploded and New Wave is here to stay.[3] Then, as the 70s gave way to the

---

1. From 'Reward' by The Teardrop Explodes, clearly.

2. The Teardrop Explodes were a bit confused in the fashion stakes. They were supposed to be New Wave but sort of dressed like Simon Le Bon before Simon Le Bon had even thought of it.

3. Well, until about 1981 anyway. New Wave was the New Punk but with less spitting.

80s, all this New Wavery morphed into New Romanticism and Julian Cope and The Teardrop Explodes were at the height of their popularity, with 'Reward' reaching number six in the UK chart. By late 1982, however, the dream was over. They split up[4] and Julian Cope went off to become a solo artist by living in Tamworth.[5]

And he had some success.[6] But as the decade wore on and he suffered various fallings out with record companies, Cope shunned the big time for a series of relatively low-key releases and tours. And then, some time round about 1991, he found himself playing a small venue in Manchester. It was a gig for about 300 people and upon arrival our intrepid New Wave pioneer noticed that above the stage was a low false ceiling, fundamentally present to mask a void of wires and beams. During rehearsal and soundcheck, the eccentric Mr. Cope expressed an interest in climbing on the speakers and getting into the space, a suggestion that

---

4. Asked if they'd ever re-form Cope famously remarked: 'Would you ever return to having your mother wipe your asshole?' Whatever that means.

5. He also went a bit mad and took too many drugs. Which at least goes some way toward explaining the whole Tamworth thing. He also became famous for his bouts of 'onstage self-mutilation, crawling around on beaches wearing nothing but a turtle shell and dressing up as a dog to "bad vibe" Margaret Thatcher out of office'.*

6. Notably with 'World Shut Your Mouth' in 1984. Not very notably since.

* Source: *Q Magazine's Greatest Rock and Pop Miscellany Ever*. I came across this lovely bit of Julian Copeness while reading it on the toilet this morning.

was quickly pooh-poohed by the crew and venue staff—firstly on the grounds of health and safety and secondly, and more importantly, on the grounds that such an idea was simply the pointless notion of an imbecile.

But then it was gig time and in front of the audience Julian dutifully climbed the speakers and got into the void from where, to the crowd's delight, he continued to sing. Then he realized he'd gotten stuck and couldn't get out. The one-time hero of the New Wave scene was now trapped in a false Manchester ceiling.

The fire brigade were called and the gig was stopped while Mr. Cope and his doubtless still pointy suede boots were rescued.

The big arse.

My Heart Will Go On, but I Won't

If there's one thing that bands hate it's a petulant roadie. But if you're on tour the rule is simple—don't piss off the road crew, because they can make your life hell.[1] When Celine Dion came to the UK in 1999 she brought with her all the flouncing, diva-like qualities[2]

---

1. They're inventive too. The crew at a stage production of *Singin' in the Rain* once all went to the toilet in the special effects rain tank high above the stage. Thus, when it 'rained' onstage certain leading members of the cast weren't so much singin' in the rain as dancin' in roadies' piss.

2. She also brought with her an entourage. Like all entourages this basically consisted of an army of simpering underlings paid to pander to her every whim. On this tour it was worse because they were all American.

that we've somehow come to expect from any Canadian whose best-known song is that one about a heart that can go on and on, despite it being located in the chest of someone who drowned when their boat hit an iceberg.[3]

Fast-forward to showtime at Wembley Stadium. With five minutes to go, in accordance with Ms. Dion's strict conditions and wishes, the backstage area is cleared of personnel so she can make her way unhindered to the stage. Her own touring crew were well aware that, even though they'd all spent the best part of a week rigging her show, Celine didn't want to catch sight of any truss monkeys, sparkies or woodpushers[4] with her own fragile eyes. Heaven forbid she meet anyone who ever does any actual work. The message was duly communicated to the on-site UK crew as well but somehow didn't reach a tiny part of the stage where a lone rigger sat near some equipment reading a newspaper.

Ahead of Celine's entrance and with 70,000 fans waiting for her, one of her 'people' did a sweep of the stage. Of course, it wasn't long before her efficient

---

3. 'My Heart Will Go On (Despite It Being Located in the Chest of Someone Who Drowned When Their Boat Hit an Iceberg)' was the (medically inaccurate) number one hit for Celine in 1997. It was the theme from the film *Titanic*, but then you knew that.

4. Basically, men (or women) with combat shorts, steel toe–capped boots and adjustable spanners. They are your crew. Respect them.

American eyes found Brit Bloke sitting on his arse covered in grime and reading the *Sun*.

'Excuse me, sir, could you leave the stage area, please?' she said.

He looks up. 'What?'

'Could you leave the stage area, only Ms. Dion is about to come past.'

'So?'

'So she likes a clear stage. She doesn't like to see anyone when she goes on.'

'Right.'

'And also her contract states that no one must look at her.'

'OK, well, I won't look at her because I'm reading the paper.'

'I'm sorry, sir, she's quite strict about this, I'm going to have to ask you to leave.'

'Well, I'm not leaving because I'm reading the paper, plus my job is to look after this stuff in case anything goes wrong.' He nods at the bank of nearby equipment.

'I'm sorry, sir, but you must leave the stage. Ms. Dion will not be looked at.'

The rigger pauses to ponder the irony of this, considering 'Ms. Dion' is about to be 'looked at' by upwards of 70,000 people, and then replies: 'Nope. I'm staying here.' He goes back to his paper.

'I'm sorry, sir, but in that case I'm going to have to call security to remove you.'

He doesn't look up. 'Off you trot then, love.'

She leaves. Nothing happens. Before long the concert is a good 15 minutes late starting and then, out of the corner of his eye, our intrepid roadie spies the woman returning, as promised, with two enormous American security guards. So he does what anyone in his position would do. He climbs ten feet up a nearby truss tower and clips himself on.

'Sir, come down and leave the stage.'

'No.'

'Sir, if you don't come down right now we will come up and get you.'

'Knock yourself out,' replies the plucky Brit and promptly climbs another ten feet.

The concert is now 20 minutes late starting. The three Americans glare at him and walk off. Another ten minutes go by before, from his lofty position where he's comfortably still reading the paper, he spies a group of people heading toward him all surrounding a tiny figure that has some cloth over its head. He climbs several feet down for a better look. Brilliantly, it's Celine Dion being walked to the stage under a blanket so she can't see him and he can't see her. He climbs a bit further down, still well out of arm's reach of anyone, and simply stares as hard as he can at her as she walks by. The fact that she doesn't even know he's doing this is irrelevant. Because of one man in his one corner of the stage that shall be forever England,

Celine Dion is both under a blanket and half an hour late for her own gig.

Rule Britannia.

The Devil in Mr. Johnson

You know what it's like. You're pottering around the house and you go to the cupboard and find that you're fresh out of souls. Dammit. And what's more, it's past eight so Sainsbury's is closed. What the devil do you do? Simple, you pop along to rural Mississippi in the 20s and try to take one from Robert Johnson.

According to legend (and even by his own admission), up until he met the Devil at a crossroads[1]

---

1. Specifically the one off US Highway 61 and US Highway 49 in Clarksdale, Mississippi. In researching this book I travelled there via Google Maps to find out what's on the site now. Unfortunately they 'don't have imagery at this zoom level for this region'. So no joy. But hey, it's America so I'm guessing to commemorate the day the Devil came to town there's now a Taco Bell, a Wendy's and a KFC. Seems appropriate somehow.

Robert Johnson was merely an average musician but, after doing a deal with the big red horny one for his soul, was granted the supernatural power of being able to play the blues.[2] But did he really have the Devil to thank? Well, let's examine the facts because, for me, the legend doesn't quite ring true. Quite *why* the Dark Lord Beelzebub, Lord of All Lies, would visit this mortal plane and, rather than lead the screaming masses back into the very gaping maw of Hades itself, would choose instead to just hang round a busy road junction simply isn't clear. I mean, why take one soul when you can probably pick up hundreds from those aforementioned screaming masses in one fell swoop?[3] Although, on the other side of the argument, it is true that after his supposed satanic trade-off Johnson began to write songs with titles like 'Hellhound on My Trail' and 'Me and the Devil Blues', suddenly becoming possibly the single most influential musician of all time. But then, after precisely 29 of these songs, he died under mysterious circumstances.[4]

Of course, the Devil has long had an association

---

2. Or, at the very least, play 'Layla' without looking at the guitar tabs book.

3. In rural folklore it is said that the intersection of two roads is an evil place and thus the Devil was able to manifest himself there. I think it's more likely that the Devil had claimed asylum seeker status and was hanging round near the traffic lights washing windscreens for a buck.

4. Allegedly killed by whiskey poisoned by the jealous husband of a lover. Or maybe he went to Taco Bell or Wendy's.

with music. He doesn't just turn up at road junctions. Sometimes, like some sort of less foul and hellish Simon Cowell, he gets involved in music competitions as well. In 1979 he famously went down to Georgia for a fiddling competition with the Charlie Daniels Band.[5] Sadly, according to the song, he lost, but as he'd given up the violin after Grade 2 at school, he's only got himself to blame. He was due back on this Earth most recently on June 6, 2006,[6] but failed to show up. It was a Tuesday and all that happened was that *Holby City* was on as usual and I had to remember to put the recycling bags out.

But did the Devil do a deal for Robert Johnson's soul and then kill him? Who knows, but if you're reading this book, Satan,[7] why not pop back? I'm sure we can come to some arrangement over Sting.

---

5. See (or rather hear) 'The Devil Went Down to Georgia' from the album *Million Mile Reflections*.

6. Because it was the 6th of the 6th of the 6th. 666. The number of the beast. Although June 6, 2006, was actually 662006 so all that showed up was a crappy remake of *The Omen*.

7. Probably on the toilet like everyone else is.

The Best to You Each Morning

Breakfast cereals. We've all had them. In our house, when I was a child, it was a relatively simple affair. Weetabix, porridge, Corn Flakes. But sometimes for a treat, or if we were going on holiday camping in Wales, we'd have one of those Kellogg's Variety packs as a treat.[1] You remember Variety packs? Of course you do, because you can still get them.[2] They were—and are—eight small versions of the original full-size packets of

---

1. Every year we spent a week in a trailer tent in a wet field near Dolgellau. To be fair, under those circumstances, anything would seem like a fucking treat.

2. I imagine Peter Kay will remember them. He's a remembering genius. He remembers garlic bread and everything. Genius, I tell you.

94

cereal except priced significantly higher by wheat marketing executives. If you're internet savvy, think of them as breakfast thumbnails. But the childhood miracle of the Variety pack was made complete because in with the boring old Corn Flakes and run-of-the-mill Frosties were edible flakes of excitement like Ricicles, Cocoa Pops and Rice Krispies. Thus this livened up the most boring of breakfasts and we were happy children. All of which brings me rather neatly to Pete Townshend.[3]

Yes, this is the story of Pete Townshend and his Corn Flakes, with specific reference to how he used to use them to annoy hotel staff that had fallen foul of him.[4] You see the thing about Corn Flakes, as anyone who has ever had a bowl and then not washed it up straight away will know, is that when left in that state they form a yellow crust around the edge of a bowl that is approximately equivalent to the thickness and toughness of the Earth's mantle. Even industrial sanding and/or drilling equipment cannot shift the iron residue of those dried-on and neglected golden flakes

---

3. Not the idea of children, you understand. I am happy to reiterate that Mr. Townshend was innocent of any crime. He simply received a caution for 'researching a book'. When's it coming out, do you think?

4. In what ways we are not sure. Perhaps they were miffed with him because he regularly enjoyed smashing a 1952 Cherry Sunburst Gibson Les Paul Deluxe into a bellhop.*

* He never did this.

of corn. Thus, armed with this, the arcane knowledge of a thousand students, Mr. Townshend would, throughout his stay, go ahead and order bowlfuls of Kellogg's on room service. Lots of bowlfuls. Packets of the stuff. Mr. Kellogg could have retired on the profits, if only he wasn't dead. But Pete wouldn't eat them, oh no. He had much better cornflakey plans. This is Pete Townshend we're talking about and only he can induct Corn Flakes into the rock 'n' roll hall of wrongness.

Thus, on the day before checking out of the hotel he would put the plug in the bathroom sink and fill it with Corn Flakes, milk and sugar like it was some sort of giant bowl.[5] This he would leave for a while and then pull the plug to get rid of the milk. He would next methodically turn the heating up for 24 hours and then leave. The resulting solid mass of rock-hard riboflavin and thiamin B1 would thus be harder to penetrate than Charlotte Church in the years before she met that chav from the nearby estate. I have heard rumors that various luxury hotels around the world still bear the Corn Flake scars of a visit from Townshend. If you're ever in one, look around the rim of the sink carefully and you may witness a little crusty bit of yellowing rock history.

Still, at least he didn't shit in the hair dryer.[6]

---

5. Which, to be fair, it is.

6. See 'Shit Hot', in this very book.

No Sleep 'til Dresden

At his house in Willesden, Lemmy out of Motorhead[1] has dozens and dozens of Airfix models of German bombers. Why this comes as no great surprise to anyone I'm not sure, but it could have something to do with Motorhead's by now legendary appearance onstage in Dresden[2] in 1979. As part of their tour

---

1. Let's face it, Lemmy Kilmister isn't 'out of' Motorhead. Lemmy Kilmister *is* Motorhead. The other blokes are called ... er ... thingy and y'know, the other one. Also, quite, quite brilliantly, Motorhead were originally called 'Bastard'. They apparently had to drop this name when told that Phil Collins had kind of cornered the whole 'being called bastard' thing.

2. War fact: On Valentine's Day in 1945 Dresden was carpet-bombed by the RAF in one of the most controversial events of the Second World War.

Lemmy had been experimenting with various fancy stage accoutrements: lights, flashing lights, new moustaches, new warts, new flashing warts and great big speakers the approximate size and weight of whatever city they were playing in,[3] but, above all this, high above the stage, they hung a life-size replica of a Lancaster bomber. We'll come back to this in a moment, but first, some background.

Lemmy is obsessed with Anglo-German relations, specifically the parts of that special relationship where we used to blow each other up. Hence the 60-something man's ceilings are festooned with Airfix models just like mine was when I was ten.[4] He also famously collects Nazi memorabilia like a plughole might collect

---

3. Motorhead hold the Guinness world record for 'Loudest Band on the Planet'. This is because they are the loudest band on the planet.

4. My ceiling wasn't all German bombers though.* In fact my favorite was a model of the Angel Interceptor from *Captain Scarlet*. It stood out against the greys of the Jaguar fighters and the greens of the F11 Mirages because it was bright white, as all good Angel Interceptors are supposed to be. It was clearly part of the same family though because, like all the other models, it was simply a mess of Airfix 'cement' (i.e. glue), misaligned and torn transfers that had gone wrong the moment I'd floated them in a saucer of water to get them off the backing paper, and yes, of course you couldn't see into the cockpit because the cack-handed application of said 'cement' had rendered it completely opaque. Airfix models. Do you remember them? Remember? Oh tits, hang on, I appear to have turned into Peter fucking Kay.

* For some reason, completely defying the laws of gravity and/or logic, I also had an Airfix model of a battleship hanging up there. No idea why.

hair. This hobby has led to him being accused of having extreme right-wing tendencies[5] but, to be honest, rather than this being an indication that he advocates genocide or the rise of an Aryan race, it seems he actually just likes the uniforms. In an interview with New York's *Waste Music* in 2004 he said:

The bad guys always had the best uniforms. Napoleon, the Confederates, the Nazis. They all had killer-uniforms. I mean, the SS-uniform is fucking brilliant! They were the rock stars of that time. What you gonna do, they just look good. Don't tell me I'm a Nazi 'cause I have uniforms.

He's right as well. The more inherently evil you are the smarter your uniform. After all, the staff in Tesco look very presentable, don't they, but we all know that as a company they're on the verge of acquiring nuclear capability. Critics have also noted the Iron Cross that Lemmy has encrusted onto his bass guitar, but so what? Just because a man chooses to have the symbol of the German armed forces and thus, by association, the Holocaust, on his rhythm instrument that doesn't make him a Nazi. So what if the man who wrote 'Orgasmatron' and 'Killed by Death' is the proud owner of an SS dagger and a rare Damascus Luftwaffe sword, worth at least $10,000? What exactly

---

5. Like Hitler. Or Kilroy.

is your problem with the self-proclaimed anarchist thinking that at least some of the Holocaust may have been exaggerated and professing his admiration for Hermann Goering by saying:

He's the only one I admire at all, in part because the portly Luftwaffe chief set up the Gestapo, the Nazis' secret police, and took the blame when he went on trial at Nuremberg after the war. His suicide, hours before he was due to be hanged, was fantastic.[6]

You see? Lemmy is just a man with a keen sense of humor. Which brings us neatly back to that Lancaster bomber that we left dangling above the stage on the German leg of the Motorhead Bomber Tour. Lemmy and the band walked out to kick off their first number. The lights come up illuminating the vast British war machine perched high above.

'Good evening, Dresden,' yells Lemmy. 'I bet you haven't seen one of these for a while.'

---

6. Interview with Dogmaticblog.com, March 11, 2005.

Fleetwood Crack

I'm not going to beat around the bush but rather I'll just come out and say this one: Stevie Nicks out of Fleetwood Mac used to like nothing more than to have cocaine blown up her arse with a straw.

Right. That's done. But now let's rewind. It will come as no surprise, and hopefully nor as legal proceedings, to learn that Ms. Nicks in her heyday was fairly partial to the odd snifter of the powdery rock talc, and this led, Danniella Westbrook–like,[1] to the deterioration

---

1. Danniella Westbrook: Actressy tabloid magnet whose nose fell out due to heavy cocaine use.

of her septum, leaving a hole in her nose through which it was possible to fit Mick Fleetwood sideways.[2]

OK, so we've established that cocaine was destroying her nose, but if you're mental for the stuff I guess needs must and so it was that, according to popular mythology, she quickly had the bright idea to alter the drug's site of ingress into her body and from then on got a roadie to blow it up her backwards area with a drinking straw.

It must be said before we go any further that the Grand Old Duchess of Rock denied this story in an interview in 2001, suggesting the very notion was 'absurd', but hey, let that not stop us from speculating. To be fair to Ms. Nicks though, the whole arse/straw thing does seem like an enormous amount of effort to go to. I mean, first, you've got to find a straw. How often is a drinking straw handy? I've never owned any and the only places I can think of where you'd find one in a hurry are on the counter in McDonald's or in a school playground stuck to the side of a child's small cardboard box of Um Bongo.[3] Both of these places seem ever so slightly inappropriate as the sort of place

---

2. And that's not easy. At over 6′ 5″ he's the Peter Crouch of music. Plus his beardy face would surely tickle.

3. Contrary to popular belief, they don't drink it very much in the Congo. Children's packed-lunch favorites are surprisingly difficult to get hold of in an equatorial western African democratic republic.

to start to get some cocaine blown up your arse so already one begins to agree with Stevie and her own doubts about the validity of the tale. And then there's the blower himself. Assuming that you are the willing 'blowee' and not put off by the close proximity of large fries or synthetic tropical fruit drink, you still have to persuade a 'blower' to put their pursed lips somewhere in the vicinity of your anus (while it's got a straw up it) and blow. Plus, the straw (I'm guessing) needs to be filled with cocaine prior to starting otherwise the whole process is going to take quite a while because the angles would be all wrong. Not to mention, before you've even got your pants off, there's a good chance the patrons of McDonald's will have called the manager, and the children, who are now unable to drink their Um Bongo because you've nicked their straw, will call the police.

So it's a logistical nightmare. I'd further venture that the blower is someone you'd quite want to trust. For a start they're going eye to (brown) eye with your arse and given that the average length of a drinking straw is what, six inches?, I'm thinking that you wouldn't want a stranger up there. Also, a stranger might not worry too much about how far the straw went in, which may well cause more issues further down the line. So, taking all that into consideration, let's assume the blower is a friend, the straw's sharp edges are being carefully handled, the diners and the children aren't looking and the drugs have been preloaded into the barrel of the straw. Then—and only then—can the blowing commence. But do you blow it all up in one go? Or is it several short, sharp blows? Can you suck a bit in for yourself as blower's privilege, a task surely fraught with its own dangers? To be honest, the whole thing is a potential minefield. Well, not literally. I hardly think it's the sort of thing Princess Diana would have volunteered to be the charitable face of.

So with all the evidence of lips and straws before us I think we should believe Stevie Nicks when she says it's just an absurd rumor. I am happy to state for the record that I believe the Nicks arse to remain unsullied by anything other than those materials for which it was intended.

Although of course there's also that version of the story involving the use of a hollow Biro casing and a hand fan . . .

Blondie: Portrait of a Serial Killer

She was the punk queen of the late 70s, a superblonde pin-up and rude fantasy of a thousand teenage boys. But, according to the lady herself, she was nearly none of these things because one summer's evening on Manhattan's East Side she was almost kidnapped and murdered by the notorious serial-killing nutbox Ted Bundy.[1]

This is a story that Debbie Harry told to ABC television in 2003. She claims that she was living in New

---

1. By all accounts, not a very nice chap at all. Angry, frightening and dangerous. A bit like Van Morrison with a knife.

York in the early part of that decade, before she was famous, and one night ... hang on ... why should I do all the work? Here's what she said:

I was being, you know, a bad girl, I s'pose. I was up late and I was trying to get across town to a party and it was two or three o'clock in the morning and then ...

Actually she goes on and on like this for a while. There's a bit about the type of shoes she was wearing and then we get to a bit where a car keeps driving past her before offering her a ride. She says no several times and then, because she can't see a cab, she agrees. Let's rejoin her:

And I got in the car and, um, the, uh ... the windows were all rolled up, and it was summertime and it was really hot. And this guy had an incredibly bad, you know, smell to him. He smelled really awful. And I looked over at the window, just, you know, sort of with my eyes[2] and the window was open about this much at the top and, um, it was a little car, a little white car. And then, uh, I looked down at the door 'cause I was going to crank open the window, and there were no door handles and no cranks. And then I started scanning the inside of the car and there was absolutely nothing. The inside of the car was completely stripped and I just ... the hair on the back of my neck just stood up.

---

2. As opposed to with what, Debbie? Your tits?

And I just said, 'Uh-oh', and I got . . . I wiggled my arm out the window and opened the door from the outside. I don't know how I did it but I got out. I threw myself out into the street, almost got run over by a cab. That cab, I wanted that cab. Where was that cab when I needed it?[3]

Blimey. Did her mother not tell her never to accept lifts from strangers? Particularly the ones who've removed all the door handles and smell of death? Debbie also said that she only realized it was mental old Bundy when, years later, she read of his description and methods of abduction[4] in newspapers. Of course, in the interests of fair play it should be pointed out that many dispute that Blondie[5] ever met Bundy. According to police records Bundy never even visited New York, preferring to be hell-bent on crazy killing in Salt Lake City and Florida. The police also say that at no time did he ever drive a stripped-out car and the only modification he made to his VW[6] was 'to

---

3. Interview with Andrew Denton on *Enough Rope*, ABC Television, August 18, 2003.

4. Again, I'm not doing all the work for you. I'm not Wikipedia. For more info see The Internet.

5. Yes, I do know that Blondie was the name of the band and not her. I just like alliteration.

6. Now owned by Jonathan Davies, lead singer of Korn. He bought it when it was auctioned off by police. I didn't know they did that with old criminal evidence. That's good news. That means that in the future there's

occasionally remove the passenger seat to enable him to carry "cargo" '.[7]

Still, One Way or Another, Picture This: *whoever* she met In The Flesh, at least he didn't Rip Her to Shreds.[8]

---

a slim chance I can get my hands on that Gary Glitter wig that I've always wanted.

7. *Shudder* From police report quoted on the excellent myth-busting website Snopes.com.

8. If you think you can come up with any more than four poor-quality and tenuous serial-killing/song title puns by simply combining the possible murder of Debbie Harry with Blondie lyrics then why not send them to me, c/o Penguin Books. You could win a cash prize.*

* You couldn't.

Papa's Got a Brand-New Bag

And so he may have, but I bet it's not the same as the one Sir Cliff Richard has supposedly got. You see, the Peter Pan of Pop is also reputedly the Peter Pan of Poo, as rumor says, some years ago, he was fitted with a colostomy bag.

Whether he was or wasn't, it's sort of beside the point here because clearly, from this story, several of the crew working on the BBC's now axed *Top of the Pops* were under the impression that Lord Cliff of Christ was fully bagged up and decided, possibly after a long crew members' lunch,[1] to see how many times, for their

---

1. Possibly in a long crew members' bar.

own amusement, they could 'subtly' refer to the bag directly to Cliff's face during rehearsal without him noticing.[2] The gauntlet was thrown down, the baton was picked up and the bag was under verbal attack.

'Cliff,' came the opening gambit from a cameraman. 'Could you just move to your left a bit, I need to bag a tight shot.' Oh yes. Good start. Who's next?

'Sorry, Mr. Richard, just need to stop for sound. We're picking up a cleaner's Hoover. Can someone go and tell the old bag to stop?' Nice one. Tight and effective.

But then there's a straight comeback re the cleaner from the floor manager: 'She says she'll stop in a minute. She's got to go and empty the bag.' Oh yes, top work from floor management. *Empty* the bag. Surely that's a bonus point?

'Sorry to take so long with the rehearsal, Cliff, my fault, I'll probably get the sack.' Oh, what a disappointment there from the young lighting guy. *Nul points*, a sack just isn't the same as a bag.

But hang on, here comes another one from the camera department and it's a devastatingly clever swift one-two: 'Cliff, did you ever do *The Tube*?' There it is!

---

2. Details of which song Sir Cliff was performing are sketchy. It was either 'Mistletoe and Wine' or that one where he sort of sang the Lord's Prayer for no discernible reason.

Whammo! I can smell victory.[3] But then there's a final last-ditch entry from the director in the gallery, who they didn't even know was playing: 'Thanks, everyone, another one in the bag.' Yes! We. Have. A. Winner!

Ah, the joshing humor of the crew. They are genuinely a credit to the entertainment industry and I hereby salute them. Cliff of course failed to notice anything and, being the consummate professional, simply complied with the wishes of the technical staff and was on his way. You might think he's blissfully unaware of the colostomy bag rumor but far from it. To his credit and with good grace it's denied on his official website. 'Cliff has never had stoma surgery,' it reads, 'this story has been doing the rounds for years but is totally unfounded.' Indeed there have been no actual proven sightings of Cliff's bag; in that sense it remains very much the Loch Ness Monster of all functional stool-draining receptacles.

Recently I told this story to a cameraman, who posited yet another theory. Perhaps Cliff *has* had surgery but, through intensive research, has designed a single meal containing all the nutrients his body will need during the day. He eats this every morning and has worked out when it will start to exit his body. This way he doesn't have to have his bag attached all day.

---

3. At least, given the subject, I hope it's victory.

Clever. He is able then, according to this new evidence,[4] to remain wired only for sound, not for shit.

Cliff, it's over to you.

---

4. Of course, it's not evidence and should be treated as not evidence until anyone proves otherwise. If you're a member of any kind of technical crew and have worked or are soon to be working with Sir Cliff, why not see what you can find out. Write to 'Sir Cliff Richard's Colostomy Bag: The Evidence', c/o Penguin Books.

Games Without Frontiers

And it's to a frontier we travel, specifically the East German one in 1985 and, even more specifically, to the border with Poland, an area where Talk Talk,[1] somewhat inexplicably, are at the height of their pop star powers.[2] Yes, in 1984/85, with the release of their *It's My Life* album, Talk Talk were huge in Eastern Europe,

---

1. For the benefit of younger readers I'm clearly referring to the band, not the mobile phone network. Or 'mbl phn ntwk' as you probably call it.

2. Although it should be pointed out in all fairness that, comparatively, the height of Talk Talk's pop star powers was about 4′ 2″, which is medically a dwarf.

making them roughly as popular as the sex trafficking industry is today.

The band is on tour and, on this leg, are about to pass through the East German border. It's at a time when the Berlin[3] Wall is still up, the Cold War is still chilling this part of the world and, as a result, the border is still populated by suspicious border control officers whose grasp of the whole 'pop star' thing is roughly equal to the grasp that the Germans still have of table manners.[4]

So as Talk Talk head through customs they are disappointed but not altogether surprised when they are taken to one side for questioning by the guards. German customs officials in 1985 may well have been unfamiliar with the inner workings of anything in the music industry that wasn't Kraftwerk, but were, it seems, of the opinion that if anyone was likely to be muleing drugs across a border then it was bound to be a progressive

---

3. For the benefit of older readers I'm referring to the capital city of Germany, which was split by a separation barrier (conceived by the East German administration of Walter Ulbricht and approved by Soviet leader Nikita Khrushchev) that closed the border between East and West Berlin for a period of 28 years and was built during the post–Second World War period of divided Germany in an effort to stop the drain of labor and economic output associated with the daily migration of huge numbers of professionals and skilled workers and the attendant defections, which had political and economic consequences for the Communist Bloc—and not the band Berlin, who did that shit ballad from *Top Gun*.

4. Casual racism. Why not? Doesn't harm Jeremy Clarkson's sales.

New Wave synth act from the south-east of England.

Almost at once, then, Mark Hollis, chief songwriter and lead singer, is separated from the others and taken into one of those clinically suspicious side rooms where you just know that something sterile is about to happen. Predictably and with the efficiency of the German men in uniform who had generationally preceded him, the customs officer instructs Mark to remove his clothes and assume the position that we have all come to know as 'bent over'.

'So,' comes the cold German steely voice from behind him, 'you are in a "pop" band?'

Without waiting for an answer there is the 'snap' of a rubber glove being administered to a hand.

'Oh ja, we know of your so-called "pop" bands over here.'

Mark, understandably given his assumed position, did not feel this warranted a reply. He felt the officer move closer.

'There is one question I wish to know the answer to,' continued the German Customs and Excise Service's answer to Herr Flick.[5]

---

5. Herr Flick. You remember. From TV's *'Allo 'Allo!*, the hilarious comedy set during the German occupation of France and designed to wring all of the comedy it could from the hilarious time when 1.25 million French troops and countless civilians had been killed by occupying German forces. It starred the actor Gorden Kaye, who once got hit in the face by a log. Is he still alive, Gorden Kaye? I can't remember.

Mark tensed and yes, there it was. The probing finger was slid in. As it reached in as far as it would go and was quite possibly as uncomfortable as it could be, the customs officer asked the question he'd been building to throughout this whole degrading experience. With his finger firmly ensconced in a pop star and with no trace of emotion whatsoever he simply asked: 'Do you know Peter Gabriel?'

Never has the outcome of any given situation depended on the right answer to a question as much as that one did. Records do not state what the correct answer was. All we know is that, after a while, Talk Talk were allowed to continue on their way.

Too Young to Live, Too Fat to Fly

On August 25, 2001, just 17 days before Osama bin Laden played Giant Jenga with the Twin Towers, another tragically fatal plane incident took place. This one, however, was less to do with international terrorism and more to do with being fat.

It was a sunny day and 22-year-old R&B star Aaliyah was en route from the Bahamas to Miami in a twin-engine Cessna, a light aircraft specially designed not to carry nine people, a ton of luggage and a pilot full of cocaine and alcohol who wasn't even actually licensed to fly the thing in the first place.[1]

---

1. The pilot, Luis Morales III, wasn't registered with the FAA, had falsely obtained his licence and simply hadn't flown anywhere near the amount of hours he claimed. Plus, an autopsy revealed high levels of cocaine and alcohol in his blood. The clown.

Aaliyah's star, unlike her plane, was rising. She'd just finished filming the video for her latest single, 'Rock the Boat', appeared in *Romeo Must Die* alongside Jet Li and had almost completed the lead role in the movie *The Queen of the Damned*, based on the Anne Rice novel. Her song 'Are You That Somebody' had also just been featured on the soundtrack to the Eddie Murphy film *Dr. Dolittle* but, despite that setback, she wasn't doing too badly at all until, at the southern end of runway 27 on Abaco Island, the answer to the age-old question as to who had eaten all the pies became all too painfully clear. It seemed that Aaliyah's two enormous bodyguards had.

Basically, the small plane was dangerously overloaded and, thanks to Tweedledum and Tweedlefatbastard, as it took off it simply couldn't gain any altitude. As a result it just nosedived into some marshland and everyone onboard was killed. An investigation—and subsequent testimony from a baggage handler[2]—revealed that Aaliyah's minders were so big that they didn't fit up the aisle of the plane. Consequently, they'd sat at the back, directly over the luggage compartment, which was already dangerously overloaded with bling. Two fatties + bling + coked-up pilot = crash.

---

2. Incidentally, someone once told me that, contrary to the slogan above the entrance to John Lennon Airport in Liverpool that reads 'Above us, only sky', the baggage handlers therein have their own motto: 'Imagine, no possessions'.

Nowadays, as a direct result of both this incident and the events of 9/11, US airlines have issued a list of undesirables who are no longer allowed to fly. They include any Muslims whose names have been linked with terror organizations as well as Pavarotti, the kid off the front of the Fatboy Slim album and Eamonn Holmes.

'I Said No Squeaks!'

Having completed, and had tremendous success with, the *Off the Wall* album, Michael Jackson was recording the follow-up, *Thriller*, in a Los Angeles studio sometime in 1982. The producer was Quincy Jones, legendary impresario, trumpet player and multiple Grammy winner of multiple Grammies. All of which doesn't explain why, when an engineer walked into the studio where the *Thriller* sessions were taking place, he found the man responsible for Will Smith's career[1] and who

---

1. True. Quincy Jones Entertainment produced *The Fresh Prince of Bel Air*, which put comedian/rapper/actor Will Smith on the map. Still, being on the map isn't necessarily a good thing. For instance, I've got a *Road Atlas of Great Britain* that has a bit of coleslaw out of a Ginsters Buffet Bar on it. It's been there for ages and has gone solid.

was childhood friends with Ray Charles[2] frenziedly yelling and screeching like a man possessed at a pile of rags on the floor. And every so often he would pause, cease yelling and screeching and switch to screaming instead, bending down and blaring at the rags: 'Do it *silent*, you motherfucker! I said NO SQUEAKS!'

After a while it became clear that the bundle of rags was actually a whimpering Michael Jackson. They had been in a long session trying to record a brand-new song called 'Billie Jean' and Michael had decided to fill every gap with his trademark clicks and whoops and gibbering noises. Quincy, for his part, wanted the track to be whoop-free. It transpired that after hours and hours of trying to get the melty-faced pop mannequin to stop his jabbery howling, Quincy had finally snapped and quite simply lost it with the waxy King of Pop.

After the verbal kicking, Jackson sang the song exactly as Quincy had wanted. Any yammering sounds on the rest of the *Thriller* album were probably just the result of Jacko sobbing into the fur of that tiger cub that was on the cover. ★*Grabs crotch*★ Yooow.

---

2. The blind singer. Not, as I thought at first glance, the 'hilarious' ventriloquist from the 70s. That turns out to have been Ray *Allen* and *Lord* Charles. And neither of those two is blind. Shit, yes, but not blind.*

* Technically Lord Charles *was* blind on the grounds that he was a big wooden doll. But he had a monocle. So it's confusing.

Bring Me a Gun, Mr. Piano Man

Jerry Lee Lewis, it must be said,[1] had much in common with one Elvis Aaron Presley. For a start they were both signed to Sun Records, for a second start they could both lay claim to being the true fathers of rock 'n' roll and for a third start they were both druggy madmen who came delightfully close to meeting at Graceland one warm Memphis morning, at about 3 a.m.

Have you seen *The Lord of the Rings*? The first or second one, I can't remember which, but it's the one

---

1. To be fair this is an exaggeration. It doesn't need to be said at all. I'm only saying it by way of an introduction.

where the Bad Goblins, or whatever they're called, lay siege to the fortress of Helm's Deep. They begin to batter its turrets with rocks and catapults the size and shape of rocks and catapults, all the while bellowing at the sky like angry tramps. Well, imagine that but instead of the Goblins think Jerry Lee Lewis. And instead of Helm's Deep think the gates of Graceland in Memphis, Tennessee, and instead of rocks and catapults think a Lincoln Continental driven by a piano-playing mental. The bellowing at the sky thing though, that can stay.

Yes, out of his mind on a cocktail of drugs and 13-year-old-cousin sex,[2] the story goes[3] that Lewis rocked up to the gates of Graceland and, rather than politely knock and announce his arrival, instead began to ram said gates with his massive car while a loaded derringer rattled about on the dashboard. And then the afore-mentioned bellowing at the sky started: 'Tell Elvis the Killer is here!' he yelled over and over and over and over and over again. 'Tell Elvis the Killer is here!'

---

2. He had a penchant for this sort of thing did Jerry. He actually even famously married his underage cousin of course. Perfectly acceptable in the rural South of Bible Belt America, terribly frowned upon in England. Apart from in Cornwall, obviously. Haha. That's right, I made a pedophiliac incest joke at the expense of the people of Cornwall. Thank you very much, ladies and gentlemen, I'm here all week, try the lazy-comedy-stereo-type-flavored veal.

3. Catalogued brilliantly in Nick Tosches's Jerry Lee Lewis biography *Hellfire* (Avalon, 1982).

Security simply called the police, who arrested him and took him away in handcuffs. It was politely explained to Mr. Lewis that Mr. Presley saw no one at 3 a.m. unless that someone was delivering prescription drugs and/or three or four skipfuls of Nutella and as Sir was simply trying to smash Mr. Presley's gates down and kill him he would have to come back at a more reasonable hour.

He never did. Years later, when Elvis died of hamburger cancer, Jerry Lee was asked for a comment. 'Good,' he said. 'I'm glad he's dead. Just another one out of the way. I mean, Elvis this, Elvis that. What the shit did Elvis do except take dope I couldn't git a-hold of?'

The day after the Graceland incident, Jerry Lee went to the hospital and was diagnosed with a peptic ulcer. At the time of writing he is still alive. Elvis, depending on who you talk to, isn't.

New Sensation

It's a biggie this. And I couldn't let the book pass without giving it a quick mention. That's right, you remember, it's the one about Michael Hutchence wanking himself to death.[1]

I'll keep it brief. At around lunchtime on November 22, 1997, a housekeeper at the Ritz Carlton in Sydney entered the INXS lead singer's room and found him hanging naked from the back of the door by a leather belt. The floor of the room was apparently covered in

---

1. Although maybe he didn't. Certainly the coroner didn't think so, recording a verdict of suicide.

empty bottles of alcohol and bottles of prescription drugs, not to mention photographs of his girlfriend Paula Yates.[2] He was 37.

Well, it was complicated. Hutchence had embarked on an affair with Yates while she was still married to scruffy famine and poverty abolisher Sir Bob Geldof[3] and she'd famously moved out of the family home with her and Bob's daughters, Ra Ra Rasputin, Lemsip and Aviary. A vicious custody battle over the children had then developed and it was perhaps the stress of all this, suggested the coroner's verdict, that led Hutchence (with whom by now Yates had had a child[4]) to commit suicide.

But soon other details began to emerge. Reports suggested that the evening before he was found decorating a door with himself, Hutchence had had a blazing row with Geldof on the phone. Then the 'photos of Paula' story leaked out, leading to speculation that he'd been masturbating over pictures of his girlfriend and that his

---

2. Paula, refusing to accept that he would have killed himself, fought to have the suicide verdict overturned, which, slightly bizarrely, suggests she would have been happier with a verdict of wanking himself to death. Sadly she herself died from an overdose in September 2000.

3. She was quoted, when talking about the illicit sex marathon circa 1996, as saying something along the lines of 'some of the things Michael taught me I'm sure were illegal'. No idea what these were though. Could have been anything from council tax evasion to happy slapping.

4. Born 1996. Christened Chitty Chitty Bang Bang.

death had been the result of an act of autoerotic activity that had gone horribly wrong.[5] Another report[6] at the time stated that Paula had been overheard telling passengers on her subsequent flight to Australia that Bob Geldof had murdered Hutchence to stop her from marrying him, a remarkable feat given that a) Geldof wasn't even in Australia at the time and b) with his level of uncleanliness, he'd have left DNA and strands of hair all over the place.

Perhaps we'll never know the truth about what happened that night, nudey photographs of Paula or not. Even with all the speculation above, still others speculate[7] that considering his other girlfriends had included Kylie Minogue and Helena Christensen, Michael's choice of visual stimuli on this occasion must have really been the act of a desperate man.

Whatever the truth, we can be sure that poor hotel housekeeper came face to face that day with a very different kind of tip than the one she'd been expecting.[8]

---

5. This is where you have a gentleman's wrist adventure while simultaneously cutting off your own air supply. The theory being that choking to the point of unconsciousness during ejaculation heightens sexual pleasure. The reality being that you end up hanging off the back of a hotel door like a hairy dead dressing gown.

6. Source: www.chartattack.com. Daily Music News, November 24, 1997.

7. Somewhat cruelly if you ask me.

8. Hahahahahaha. Yeh it's a nob gag. So what? Hutchence started it.

One (Pissed) Man Went to Mow

Lawnmowers have not, for me, played a big enough part in the annals of rock. Lawns themselves have—after all, the drummer from Toto died the most rubbish rock 'n' roll death ever when it transpired that he was allergic to weedkiller and fell over on the grass while tending to his roses.[1] But the lawnmower's role in musical history is unimpressive. With one notable exception.

As if living a real-life dramatization of one of their

---

1. As comedian Rich Hall brilliantly puts it: 'He fought the lawn, and the lawn won.'

own songs, married couple and Lord and Lady of Country Music George Jones and Tammy Wynette had their ups and downs. Being of, and from, a world that relies on the slide guitar and the fiddle for entertainment, I imagine that everything bad that could befall such a marriage had already happened to George and Tammy; everything from shootin' a man in Reno just to watch him die to begging you to please don't take my man—both of which, as marital circumstances go, would certainly have the potential to lead to a row.

But one day, probably after he'd been spittin' and a-fightin' in the mud and the blood and the beer, it all came to a head when George was in a particularly grumpy mood due, in no small part, to the fact that he'd been on the wagon[2] for several weeks. He was crotchety, annoyed and fed up and thus tensions beneath the surface of the Jones/Wynette marriage were simmering like Brownian motion particles caught in a line dance. So, not unreasonably some would argue, George simply decides at that moment that the wagon he's been on very much needs to be dismounted, and announces that he is driving into town for a drink.

Tammy, however, has decided that there is no way on God's clean earth that he's going to do any such thing, not with four hungry children and crops in the

---

2. Even though he's 'country' I don't think this was an actual wagon.

field,[3] and so set about hiding all five sets of car keys for all five cars that they owned. Aha! George's plan is foiled! Fortunately, their ranch is about ten miles out of town so she knows that walking isn't really an option. But, of course, George is a country singer and is therefore nothing if not resourceful. After all, if a man can ride out on a horse in a star-spangled rod-e-o then he can sure as hell hitch up his breeches and find a way to a saloon, goddammit.

So he did what any of us would do. He went on a lawnmower. He clambered aboard his ride-on lawnmower and drove at two miles an hour all the way into town, where he arrived at a bar a nifty five hours later and proceeded to get magnificently pissed. And then, when he'd had his fill of drownin' in a whiskey river, bathin' his mem'ried mind, he drove it home again. Possibly slower this time. I'd like to report that on the way back he ran over a cow, or his wife, or both, or even spent a couple of extra hours mowing the words 'Tammy is a bitch' into the family lawn so that she'd see it from an upstairs window in the morning, but sadly he didn't. Therefore, when it comes down to it, this is just the story of a pissed-up old country singer taking a painfully slow lawnmower into town and back for a drink. And you know what? In its own sweet way, it's none the worse for it.

---

3. I don't know that they had any such thing. Although I like to imagine they did because it somehow feels right.

The Myths and Legends of
King Rick and the Knights
of the Round Table

... is perhaps the longest story title in this book. It's also arguably the longest album title ever[1] and it's also arguably[2] Rick Wakeman's finest hour.[3]

1. I said arguably so let's argue. I argue that it's not. That particular accolade goes to Fiona Apple and her 1999 album *When the Pawn Hits the Conflicts He Thinks like a King What He Knows Throws the Blows When He Goes to the Fight and He'll Win the Whole Thing 'Fore He Enters the Ring There's No Body to Batter When Your Mind Is Your Might So When You Go Solo, You Hold Your Own Hand and Remember That Depth Is the Greatest of Heights and If You Know Where You Stand, Then You Know Where to Land and If You Fall It Won't Matter, Cuz You'll Know That You're Right*. She's quite, quite mad.

2. Come down here for another argument then, have you? Right then. Most would argue that *Journey to the Center of the Earth* (1974) is Rick

In 1975, while lying in the hospital, having had a minor heart attack following a performance of his previous prog-rock epic, *Journey to the Center of the Earth* ('Five days out on an infinite sea, they prayed for calm on an ocean free'[4]), and while being advised by his doctors to rest, Rick Wakeman embarked upon the epic *The Myths and Legends of King Arthur and the Knights of the Round Table*—to quote Rick: 'I wrote it in my head.'

Fair enough. Another 70s concept album, this one about the return of the once and future king. But then, quite possibly through a fug of heart drugs, Rick also begins mentally sketching out the world tour that will accompany his new album. He will take a symphony orchestra, the English Chamber Choir, a full band, the lighting, set, costumes and a spectacular Arthurian stage show of smoke and wizardry and perform the whole lot . . . on ice.

Once out of the hospital Rick set about planning his spectacle. Casting took place, wizards were recruited, dragons were tamed and the enormous ice arena that was to become the fantasy world of forests, tors, lakes

---

Wakeman's finest hour. Personally I'd argue it was when he appeared as Abanazer in Roy Hudd's *Aladdin* at a theater in Cornwall in 2001. Sample review: 'All the adults and children were happy to hiss and boo!'—*Western Morning News*. Mind you, they said the same about *King Arthur on Ice*.

3. Actually it was more like 44 minutes.

4. Not exactly Girls Aloud, is it?

and mists of Arthur and his brave knights was built at Wembley Empire swimming pool. The night of the premiere performance drew near. The crowds flocked in, shivering. Possibly with anticipation but more likely with the freezing blast of the ice refrigeration units. The moment had arrived and the Grand Keyboard Wizard Wakeman took to his mighty stage.

Only to find that all the instruments had frozen and wouldn't even switch on. It was a disaster. A funny disaster with pointy hats and cardboard swords, but a disaster nonetheless.

It is a lasting testament to its success that pretty much the only shows performed on ice nowadays are by The Tweenies.

Toxic Rock Syndrome

Briefly, some time around 1992, Latin singers became inexplicably popular outside their native country of Latin. The main exponent of this hip-rotating, rhythmic genre of nightclub lust was one Ricky Martin, who not only looked fairly impressive in a frilly shirt but also managed to pull off wearing special trousers, trousers that must have been reinforced because they had to house balls big enough to rhyme 'loca' with 'mocha'[1] and then allow their wearer to go onstage and look

---

1. As he does in *Livin' la Vida Loca*. I bet Alfred Lord Tennyson, is shitting himself in his grave.

smug about it. But Ricky Martin has every reason to look smug, for Ricky Martin is the keeper of a secret.[2]

You see, when your average performer steps out onstage under the hot, bright lights of a gig, the chances are that they're going to sweat. Even singers that don't move very much sweat onstage. Dave Gilmour out of Pink Floyd isn't noted for his scissor kicks but I've seen him with my own eyes perspiring beneath the unforgiving beam of a Varilight. Kraftwerk aren't big on choreography, but I'll wager their black German turtlenecks smell a bit in the dressing room afterward. And I imagine, when it gets under a hot bulb, the pasty skin of the mostly unmoving Liam Gallagher silently weeps raw coke. And so you can only begin to wonder what the perspiration levels of a jumping Latino groin dancer can possibly be, but I think, if we looked,[3] we'd more than likely take a moisture reading of somewhere between 'reservoir' and 'front row of a Justin Timberlake concert'.

So what to do? Wearing hand-tooled frilly shirts every night is an expensive business. No amount of antiperspirant is going to stop the river of Hispanic sweat that must emanate from the tanned torso of a

---

2. All right, it's not a great secret, I mean it's not up there with the whereabouts of the Grail or the continued employment of Justin Lee Collins but it's something quite funny. And it's not that he's gay.

3. Which we won't.

thrusting disco king, so the ever-resourceful Mr. Martin once came up with a solution. And again, it's right up there at a level of genius that we'd expect from a man who brazenly also rhymes 'Mata Hari' with 'story'[4] without a care in the world. Here we go then, his solution is this: before he goes onstage, he tapes a sanitary napkin under each arm. That's right, a couple of absorbing panty pads in the pits. He's got two armpits full of Always Ultra[5] and he's not afraid to use them. Yes it's mad but it makes sense. I mean, we've all had a shirt discolored under the arm from deodorant and Martin's menstrual makeover solves the problem. No more rings of sweat or spray under the arms and what's more you can buy whichever towel suits your flow. Ricky Martin, you are a genius with arid glands. Pity your hits dried up as well.

4. He does as well, in 'Shake Your Bon-Bon'. I mean for fuck's sake. 'Shake Your Bon-Bon'? Jesus.

5. Other sanitary products are available.

Simply the Bezst

'Manchester, so much to answer for . . .' Not my words of course but the words of bequiffed, vegetarian miserabalist Morrissey, who crooned the words on his bequiffed, vegetarian miserabalist 1984 song 'Suffer Little Children', a charming little ditty about the Moors Murders. But quite apart from being the location of Ian and Myra's Grand Day Out, Manchester was also responsible for spawning the godfathers of the 90s UK 'Madchester' scene, the Happy Mondays.

Before they went all massive[1] and when they were

---

1. Both figuratively and literally in Shaun Ryder's case.

just a minor cult, the Mondays were booked to play in front of about 200 bored students at Newcastle Polytechnic.[2] As showtime approached, all the band were there except for Shaun Ryder, the lead singer, and Bez, his dancing monkey. It transpired that their train from Manchester had been delayed but now they were in a cab racing toward the venue. The allotted time for the gig to begin came and went with still no sign of the Magnificent[3] Two and the student crowd were growing restless as the minutes ticked by. Duly, the cab firm were contacted and the driver confirmed that he'd already dropped them off at the gig. A frantic search of the Polytechnic grounds was soon underway, but even as organizers were peering into bushes for the slightest sign of Bez's maracas, a harassed and out of breath Bez and Shaun were being confronted by gig security. Hearing music onstage they gave the traditional musician's war cry of 'Let us through, we're the fucking band'[4] and charged onto the stage.

Sadly it wasn't the stage at the student union of

---

2. No longer a polytechnic of course. In common with all UK polytechnics, it is now a pretend university with ideas above its station.

3. And by 'magnificent', I mean 'fuckwitted'.

4. Up there with 'Can I have less of that twat in my monitors?' (Noel from Oasis), 'Can you send someone out for another cup of heroin?' (band name withheld for legal reasons) and 'I'm not going onstage until you get me a fucking horse whisperer like it says in my rider' (Mariah Carey).

Newcastle Polytechnic but rather the stage at the 2,000-seater Newcastle City Hall, several miles away, where Simply Red had just launched into their first number.[5]

'I thought I didn't recognize anybody,' said Bez later. An affliction, thanks to those crazy pill-popping times, that he's been stuck with ever since.

---

5. Led by Mick Hucknall, a man with the face and charm of a potato fighting to get out of a scrotum.

Billy, Don't Be a Hero

He told us he didn't want to change the world, wasn't looking for a new England, but instead was looking for another girl. Ah, the troubadourian words of Mr. Stephen William 'Billy' Bragg Esq., protest singer to the nation and all-around nice bloke.[1] Although, with his role as the angry Red Wedge troubadour at the forefront of political songwriting in the UK in the 80s, it could be argued that Billy *did* want to change the world,

---

1. Except when he's angry about stuff like social injustice, workers' rights and overzealous dry ice machines. (See 'Wet Wet Dry (Ice)' elsewhere in this book.)

was looking for a new England and, in the face of a Thatcherite junta hell-bent on destroying the unions and the working-class backbone of Britain, he probably hadn't got time for 'another girl' and would have preferred instead to be warming himself round a miner's brazier[2] and shouting at the police. Which is probably why he gave the song to Kirsty MacColl to have a hit with instead.[3]

Thus it was this fired-up and politically astute Billy that passed through a London Underground station in the late 80s only to be met by the (then) brand-new automated ticket barriers. Then, as now, these weren't without their problems[4] and Billy, the spokesman of the underclass, accosted a nearby member of London Underground staff in the ticket office.

'What the hell are you playing at with these barriers?' he ranted. 'They never bloody work, they cost a fortune, the public don't like them, your own unions don't like them and the Fire Brigade hate them because they're a fire hazard. I reckon these barriers

---

2. This is in no way a euphemism. Shame on you for thinking it was.

3. 'A New England' was on Bragg's 1983 album *Life's a Riot with Spy vs Spy*. Kirsty MacColl covered it—with Bragg having written an extra verse for her—in 1984. It's great.

4. If you've ever used the London Underground you will know that the worst two words in the English language are 'Seek Assistance'. Apart from the words 'London Underground'.

are the single biggest waste of time and money in the world.'

The uniformed employee glanced up at him. 'Write a fucking song about it then,' he said, before going back to his book.

Spinal Twat

Oasis are big. I don't mean *now* when they're still big but past their best.[1] I mean back then when 'Wonderwall' had just become an anthem to a disaffected youth—a youth who fervently believed that all the roads he had to walk were winding and that all the lights that would lead him there were blinding. It was pretentious bollocks of course but it was a great song and it was Oasis in their heyday.

Which is why, perhaps to celebrate, Noel and Liam had gone to see Spinal Tap live. *Spinal Tap* was one of

---

1. A bit like J.Lo's arse.

Liam's favorite films of all time[2] and his little northern moptop face was beaming at the prospect of seeing them onstage, live, in the flesh. And of course the gig was a belter. Two hours of pure unadulterated Tap. And then it was time for the encore. For which the Spinal Tap boys came on as A Mighty Wind.[3] The Wind begin to play a short set of their errant folk music. Liam let them get half a song in before he leaned over to his brother and said: 'Who are these cunts?'

Noel looked at him. 'It's them.'

'What?' said Liam. 'Them who?'

'*Them,*' hissed Noel.

'Them *who*?' insisted Liam.

'Fucking hell, Liam,' Noel insisted back. 'It's *them*. Spinal Tap.'

'Them's not Spinal Tap. These are some folk cunts,' eloquized Liam.

'No, Liam, it's them. It's Harry Shearer and the others. They're actors. The actors who play Spinal Tap.'

---

2. Documenting, as it does, the story of . . . hang on. Why am I telling you what *Spinal Tap* is? You know what it is. If you don't, you're reading the wrong book. Go and pick up something else. Look, over there, there's a new Martina Cole novel. It's bound to have disemboweled prostitutes in it. You like stories about disemboweled prostitutes, don't you? Weirdo.

3. Look, really, I'm not explaining it. If I have to explain then this book isn't for you. Go and browse some more. There's probably another book of Robin Cooper letters or something that'd be more up your street. Or anything by Danny Wallace.

There is a moment of silence from Liam. Even Noel must have realized what was coming next.

'*Actors?*'

And with that Liam, disgusted, walked out. It is for this reason that no one has yet told him the truth about Father Christmas.

Motley Spüe

If you're a man called Nikki Sixx (two K's, two X's) then you really do belong in a rock band. Especially one that doesn't know how to spell. Ah, Motley Crüe, how you spoil us. Even in a book that's full of rock's more glamorous tales, the zany antics of LA's finest troubadours really do cut the mustard.[1] In fact, do you know, there must be a whole book in them alone.[2] But, for

---

1. Not just cut the mustard but cut the mustard with some crack cocaine and then snort it off a stripper through another stripper.

2. Oh. There is. *The Dirt: Confessions of the World's Most Notorious Rock Band.* In their own words they 'nailed the hottest chicks, started the bloodiest fights, partied with the biggest drug dealers, and got to know the inside of every jail cell from California to Japan. They have dedicated an entire career to living life to its extreme, from the greatest fantasies to the darkest

me, one story stands out and what's more it seems to sum up the whole band in one neat, easy-to-read handy précis of a heavy metal band at the top of their game while simultaneously being at the bottom of a sewer. So brace yourself, because here we go.

The aforementioned Nikki Sixx (two K's, two X's),[3] bass player with the Crüe, and his good pal Tommy Lee[4] on the drums decided to hold a competition between them to see who could go for the longest without washing, showering or bathing in any way yet still be able to sleep with groupies without them being ill or bailing out. OK. So here are two men, sweating it out onstage every night for two hours and then sleeping, by their own admission, with maybe three or four 'chicks'. And then, at the point where most of us in that situation[5] would pop into the shower, Nikki

---

tragedies. Tommy married two international sex symbols; Vince killed a man and lost a daughter to cancer; Nikki overdosed, rose from the dead, and then OD'd again the next day; and Mick shot a woman and tried to hang his own brother.' I heartily recommend it. In many ways it's very similar in content to *If I Don't Write It Nobody Else Will*, the autobiography of Eric Sykes.

3. Real name Frank Carlton Serafino Feranna, Jr (three F's, six R's, one J).

4. Yes. That Tommy Lee. The one who married Pamela Anderson and had sex with her on a sex tape.

5. Like we all are. Well, I am. I mean I've been on Radio 2 *and* once appeared on BBC2's *I Love the 1990's*. Consequently, my life is a riot of 'whores' and 'pussy'.

and Tommy simply, erm . . . didn't. For two months. That's right. Two months of rock 'n' roll mixed with nightly groupie sex without any form of hygiene or personal grooming taking place. Just how pleasant do you imagine they were to be around?[6]

Well, hey, they're in a rock band so the groupies kept coming thick and fast.[7] The boys are neck and neck in the competition until one night, Nikki Sixx is receiving some downstairs attention from a young lady when the unclean condition of his 'Little Nikki' finally becomes too much and she gags and then vomits all over his crotch. Not only that, but her vomit is mostly strands of undigested spaghetti which all becomes tangled in Nikki Sixx's pubic hair. Naturally, rather than be embarrassed or fazed in any way whatsoever, Nikki immediately summoned Tommy Lee to the scene of the incident and conceded defeat.

In the rock band world it became known as 'The Spaghetti Incident'.[8]

Yes. Of course it did.

---

6. In other news from around this time, Ozzy Osbourne licked up a pool of Nikki Sixx's urine. Oh and both Ozzy and Nikki once snorted a line of ants. Again, if you replace the words 'Nikki Sixx' with 'Eric Sykes' and read their books, they really could be the same person.

7. Make your own joke up. I'm not doing all the work for you.

8. Also the title of a Guns n' Roses album of course. And although any connection between the two is unproven, I like to assume that one begat the other.

By Royal Appointment

What three ingredients does a good story need? Some would say a beginning, a middle and an end, but anyone who's read any of James Herbert's post–*The Fog* output will know that just because it has those three things, it certainly doesn't stop it from being bollocks.[1] So

---

1. No, I mean, really. What the hell happened to James Herbert? His recent books are rubbish. *The Rats* was great and *The Fog* had that bit in it when the PE teacher gets strung up naked in the gym to his own apparatus and then the kids cut his cock off with some shears. And this is what we were all reading when we were about ten! You don't get that in Harry Potter. Although you should: 'Professor Snape whimpered as he looked down. He was trussed so that he couldn't move, the sweat pouring from his naked body, and dripping off the end of his long nose. No spell was going to get

what else? A decent plot? Good characters? A dog called Timmy? No, what a good story needs is Ozzy Osbourne, Slash from Guns n' Roses and Sir Cliff Richard.

Imagine a room with the three of them standing together, chatting. The Prince of Darkness and Sir Christ Richard would be enough on their own but add Slash into the mix and you get an unholy trinity of truly biblical proportions. But imagine no longer because this curious meeting of minds actually happened and it was at the 2005 Royal Variety Performance in Cardiff.

Traditionally of course the artistes meet Her Majesty The Queen in a lineup after the show, where she pretends to know who they are and Prince Philip grunts at them like a racist old man. And standing together waiting to meet her on this occasion were our three unlikely bedfellows.[2]

As she gets closer, Ozzy suddenly realizes he's got absolutely no idea how to address the Queen correctly.

---

him out of this. He tried to focus and then wished he hadn't as, approaching him, he saw Harry, Ron and Hermione, their faces vacant with murderous intent. The moonlight coming in through the window glinted off something cold in Hermione's hands. With growing horror Snape realized that her dead eyes were fixed upon his manhood and it was then, and only then, as she raised the shears toward his most magic of wands, that he began to scream . . .'

2. I literally mean 'unlikely bedfellows'. By which I mean they are unlikely to share a bed at any point. Although I'm willing to gamble that a home sex tape of such an incident would be a big hit on YouTube.

He turns to ask Sir Cliff, veteran of just such auspicious occasions, exactly how one should behave when the Queen shakes one's hand.[3] Overhearing, Slash also confesses to his confrères in hushed tones that he too has absolutely no idea of the rules. An emergency training session is called for and Sir Cliff steps manfully into the breach. Thus onlookers are treated to the sight of Sir Cliff Richard teaching Ozzy Osbourne and Slash out of GnR how to shake hands, how to bow correctly and how to respectfully speak to the trout-faced old woman we call our Queen. Above all, imparts the Peter Pan of Pop, the worst thing you can ever do is turn your back on Her Majesty.

She's getting closer as Cliff begins his quick lesson but just as he gets to the important bit, Slash's young daughter decides she wants to meet the Queen as well and runs past Daddy and heads straight for the Royal legs. Slash grabs her just in time and, in trying to get her out of the way, turns round and steps out of his place in the lineup. He misses the instructions completely and of course it is at that exact second that the Queen arrives. With his wriggling daughter in one arm and a fag in the other Slash greets the Queen with his back. She, ever the consummate professional, moves immediately on to Ozzy, who mumbles a greeting, tries to remember whether it's the done thing to piss on her

---

3. It's not considered appropriate to bite the head off the Queen.

153

or not,[4] fortunately doesn't and is rescued by Sir Cliff, who does.[5] Slash meanwhile has sorted out his errant child and turns back hoping Cliff will now fully coach him in the ways of bowing, shaking hands and making idle small talk with Her Majesty. Sadly, she's long gone.

'Shit man, did I miss talking with the fucking Queen?' he asks Ozzy.

'No,' replies the wobbly one. 'He's chatting to the old dear in the hat.'

---

4. It's not. Neither is it the done thing to piss on the Texas National Monument of The Alamo but that didn't stop him from once doing it and getting arrested.

5. Of course he doesn't. His ablutions allegedly go in a bag, remember? (See 'Papa's Got a Brand-New Bag' earlier in this book.)

Snyder Remarks

In the Year of Our Lord 2005 the huge-in-the-80s heavy metal hair band Twisted Sister (lead singer Dee Snyder—half man, half makeup counter at Boots) weren't quite so big and one fine Saturday night in the provincial British town of Brighton on the provincial British south coast,[1] the rock juggernaut that was 'the Sister' hove into town.[2]

---

1. Other gigs there that season—Aha live and the National Teddy Bear Fair. Don't all rush at once.

2. Pun intended. Hove. It's near Brighton. Do you see? Never mind, forget it.

That evening, as the lights dimmed, frontman Snyder roared onto the stage and laid into the baying crowd. 'Good evening, Brighton,' he yelled through his massive cranial furball matted with smeared lipstick. 'How you doin'?' The crowd responded in the time-honored rock gig fashion by immediately roaring back the internationally recognized vocalization that translates as 'Fine, thanks, now get on with singing that one hit you had back in 1983.'[3]

But Snyder wasn't finished with his crowd-baiting just yet. 'The balcony is where all the REAL sick motherfuckers are!' he screeched as only a frontman can. 'They aren't even standing up! They can't even stand up by showtime! Let's have the house lights up to see the cunts!' When the house lights were raised, the band and audience found themselves looking up at the disabled section of the crowd, full of fans in wheelchairs.

Rock meets roll. And not in a good way.

---

3. 'I Am, I'm Me.' Honestly, it rocked.

Always on My Dad

Plant, Page, Bonham, Jones. Four men who will forever be the pilots of the Led Zeppelin. But the fifth member of the Zeps, as the kids aren't calling them, was Peter Grant, their manager and a man mountain of a management man mountain who struck terror into the hearts of all those who crossed his path. Or dared to speak to him. Or look at him. In fact I'm a bit nervous just writing his name down and *I* know that he's dead.

He was the epitome of tough management, making sure his artists got the money they deserved and that they weren't ripped off by promoters and record labels,

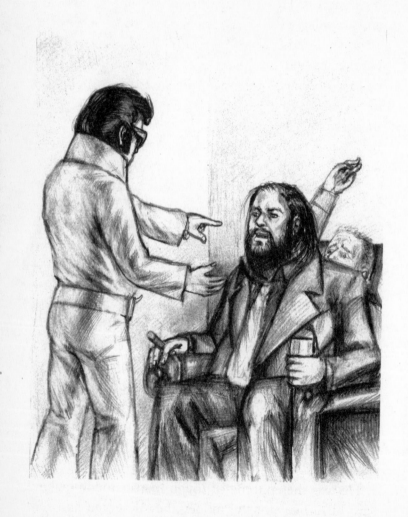

and he was instrumental in flying Led Zeppelin to their success. He was also a former bouncer, stuntman and wrestler who, at a Zeppelin gig in Vancouver in 1971, smashed up both a set of noise level monitoring equipment and the noise level monitoring equipment operator because he thought the show was being boot-legged. He would, in the words of Mark St. John, manager of The Pretty Things, 'intimidate the living hell out of people'. He was 21 stone[1] of psycho who always got what he wanted.[2]

And then one day Grant and the band were invited to meet Elvis Presley at Graceland. By this time of course Elvis had long been the King and he wanted to present Plant, Page, Bonham, Jones and Grant with engraved watches as a small token of his appreciation for where they'd taken rock 'n' roll and run with it. Elvis was a Zeppelin fan. Now that's cool. Well, it would've been except for one thing. Elvis gave them the gifts as they arrived and ushered them into his lounge. Overawed by these personal tokens from Elvis,

---

1. About 300 lb., if you're American.

2. In the late 60s he was managing Gene Vincent, who was often so drunk he wouldn't make it onstage and thus never got paid. At one gig the curtain opened to reveal Vincent with a mic stand rammed (by Grant) down the back of his jacket to hold him up. He began to sing and immediately fell forward, smashing into the stage, breaking his nose. Gig over. They got paid though. As Grant said afterward: 'I got the money because he was there when the curtains opened.'

the Zeps were invited to sit while someone fetched tea.[3] The boys duly sat, with all 300 lb.[4] of Peter Grant sinking into a large comfy-looking armchair. A minute later from the armchair there came a muffled squeak. Then another. Then another, louder, one. Everyone looked from the new watches to each other. There was another squeak. Slowly everyone looked at Peter Grant. There was another squeak and it was definitely coming from beneath him, on the chair. The enormous man, who was 80 times[5] the size of Elvis in his fat period, shrugged and struggled to get to his feet. Under him, already sitting in the chair, was Vernon Presley, Elvis's father.

Some time later, when they took their leave, Peter Grant left Elvis with these words of gratitude: 'Thanks for the watches, Elvis. Sorry I sat on your dad.'

---

3. Or Dexidrineburgers.

4. About 21 stone, if you're British.

5. About 80 times, whether you're British *or* American.

When Pop Stars Divorce

I think it was comedian Jeff Foxworthy who said that getting married for the sex is like buying a Boeing 747 for the free peanuts. They don't give you peanuts these days of course lest someone is allergic to them and explodes in midair,[1] but while this is now a strict rule, it must be said that the rules which still govern matrimony are comparatively casual. When any marriage, like that

---

1. It's just sort of salty snacks on planes these days. I think I'm right in saying that peanuts were banned on all flights after 9/11 when the passengers and crew of those hijacked planes were threatened and attacked by terrorists armed with two packets of KP dry roasted and a bag of Planter's honey cashews. (*Note to lawyers—can we check this? I may have got my facts wrong.*)

'exhausted'[2] Tom Chaplin out of Keane, breaks down, it is, of course, sad but with pop stars the inevitable dirty washing is often strewn about in public for us all to enjoy. Which makes it far more fun.

It was exciting, wasn't it, when Eric Clapton very publicly stole Patti Boyd from George Harrison, when Britney split from her first husband, Jason Alexander, after a marriage of ten minutes (and then dumped her second one, 'K-Fed', by text message), or when Paul McCartney and Heather Mills had a vicious battle over who was to get custody of the leg jokes.

But back in 1975, when soul legend Marvin Gaye split up with his wife Anna it was most definitely he who had the last laugh. They'd married in 1962, tolerated a somewhat turbulent marriage[3] and for the eventual settlement it was agreed that Gaye's wife would be entitled to all the royalties from his next album.[4]

Marvin went into the studio and emerged some

---

2. Drug-addled.

3. And by turbulent I mean that they both accused one another of infidelity. He was living with a teenage girl who he'd got pregnant and furthermore the child that he and his wife were raising was actually the result of his sexual liaison with his wife's 15-year-old niece. Turbulent. Yes.

4. Similarly, when he wrote 'You're Beautiful', bland soldier James Blunt apparently gave the rights to his then girlfriend as a token of his love. They then split up, the song was a hit and she got lots of money. Gutted.

months later with a double LP[5] full of songs of acrimonious abuse, verbal attacks and acerbic comments all about his ex.[6] Many have suggested that he deliberately made it uncommercial and difficult so that his ex would get the least amount of money possible. Others say he was just pouring his feelings out, which made it uncommercial and difficult, with the net result that his ex got the least amount of money possible. Either way, basically it was rubbish and no one bought it. Thus he wins.

So come on, McCartney, you know that revenge is a dish best eaten with a nice vegetarian pasta bake from Linda's own range. Why not follow in the footsteps of Marvin Gaye now that Heather's history? What you need to get it off your chest is make a rubbish album full of songs about her. Should be easy enough, after all I heard your last album so I know you're just about there on the whole 'rubbish' thing. All you need to do now is concentrate on the cathartic Mills material. Job done.

---

5. For those readers who may be under 30, an 'LP' is like a flat, black MP3 with two sides.

6. With his songs of spousal slagging off he was in many ways the original Eminem. Actually, not in many ways . . . just in this one way. He certainly didn't swear as much. Although I would very much like to hear a version of 'Hey Bitch, I Heard It through the Motherfucking Grapevine'.

Trying to Get Blood out of a Stone

They couldn't get any satisfaction, had sympathy for the Devil and sticky fingers, so no wonder that the world surrounding the Rolling Stones was as murky as the swimming pool in which Brian Jones bubbled his last druggy breath.[1]

But in 1973 a splendid story began to circulate about

---

1. There is much speculation as to whether he was, in fact, murdered by a builder. This seems unlikely as we all know that they rarely finish a job. 'Sorry, mate, I can't finish murdering you today—I've got another four murders on at the moment. Tea? Yep. Fifteen sugars please.' Etc. and so on and so forth in the vein of a Radio 4 lighthearted look at the week's news.

heroin-faced guitar mess Keith Richards: in order to beat his addiction to the skag he was to go into a Swiss clinic[2] and undergo a complete blood transfusion to clean up for a European tour. Let's just take a moment to think about that. A *complete* blood transfusion. All of the nasty, rancid old blood removed from his body and replaced with nice, sparkly new blood from somewhere else. It's the medical equivalent of deleting all the music from your iPod and starting again but not downloading anything by Shed Seven.

But is this story true and in any way believable to anyone other than fans of *Fantastic Voyage*?[3] Well, Keef definitely went to Switzerland in 1973 for some sort of medical treatment, but the fact is he may have just nipped over there for some fondue-flavored Strepsils because there really is no evidence to suggest he had all his plasma sucked out. No evidence at all.

Oh, hang on. No evidence that is *apart* from when

---

2. Switzerland is also the home of Dignitas, the legal suicide clinic, along with many unregistered alternative therapy centers. Why are these places always Swiss? Perhaps it's because they are a compassionate race whose desire to help people is in many ways echoed in their international reputation for neutrality toward all nations. Or, as Swiss property is a sound investment, perhaps it's simply a clever way for the cuckoo clock fiddling bunch of goatherds to launder all that Nazi gold they've been hiding.

3. The 1977 film starring Donald Pleasence and Raquel Welch. They shrank down a spaceship and injected it into the bloodstream of some bloke. See also *Innerspace*, starring Dennis Quaid. Actually no, don't.

the man himself told a journalist that it was all true and that a complete transfusion had actually taken place and it was not entirely dissimilar to being embalmed while you're still alive.

Trouble is, years later, the crazy blues-riffing buffoon said he'd been lying to the journo. 'I made it up,' he drawled with his trademark droopy mouth, 'I was just fucking sick of answering the question.'[4]

Some time later, in 2006, he fell out of a tree while scrumping coconuts. The man's a fool.

---

4. As quoted by James Sullivan in *Rolling Stone*, 2004.

Taking Libertines

Pete Doherty. What a wag. What a tip-top fellow in a jaunty hat. What a character. That's right, a character. As in 'not real'. As in made up.

According to reports that surfaced in 2006, the junkie-breathed tabloid magnet wasn't really the thieving heroin addict we'd all made him out to be. In fact he was simply the thieving heroin addict he'd been made *up* to be. His real name, it began to transpire, was Trevor McDermott and until recently he'd been making a living as a part-time Buddy Holly impersonator on the Devon and Cornwall holiday camp circuit. Some time in 2001 he'd been at a friend's party in London and got chatting to Bill Drummond and Jimmy Cauty, two former members of the KLF.[1] And the bewildered, talentless stooge had given them an idea.

The KLF, as musicians in their own right, had left the public stage very publicly indeed at the 1992 Brit Awards with the following announcement (coming just as they were stopped from pouring sheep's blood over the audience by BBC lawyers[2]):

We have been following a wild and wounded, glum and glorious, shit but shining path these past five years. The last two of which has [sic] led us up onto the commercial high ground—we are at a point where the path is about to take a sharp turn from these sunny uplands down into a netherworld of we know not what. There will be no further record releases.[3]

---

1. Late 80s/early 90s acid house collective. Hits included 'What Time Is Love?', '3 AM Eternal' and 'Last Train to Transcentral'. I remember being quite disappointed upon finding out years later that 'Transcentral' wasn't in fact the acid trip utopia I'd imagined but was instead Jimmy Cauty's nickname for his own house in Stockwell, South London.

2. Brit Awards organizer Jonathan King publicly endorsed the KLF's live performance, a response that the band's publicist, Scott Piering, cited as 'the real low point'. How prescient of Mr. Piering, given that this was years before the stroke-faced fat old goon was done for kiddy fiddling.

3. Apparently the KLF's Brits statuette for 'Best British Group' of 1992 was later found buried in a field near Stonehenge.

Christ only knows what that all meant but now in 2006 they were back! And what's more they'd brought a freak with them. Time, then, to create another of their notorious japes and pranks[4] and this one would be designed to play with the notion of celebrity culture. So it was, then, that they took the buffoon that was Trevor McDermott from Devon and turned him into something called Pete Doherty from Tosserland. Yes, the whole Libertines–Babyshambles–tales of drug use–robbery of Carl Barat's flat[5]–affair with supermodel Kate Moss[6] thing had all been part of one of the largest hoaxes in British history. 'It was meant to be,' claimed Cauty, 'a quick stunt to show the frailties of our celebrity-obsessed culture.'

Sadly though, like a fairground ride put up on a

---

4. Including setting fire to a million pounds on a remote Scottish island, firing guns at the audience at the Brit Awards and dumping a dead sheep on the floor at an aftershow party. Yeah, who hasn't?

5. 'Pete Doherty' broke into fellow band member Carl Barat's flat to steal stuff to pay for his smack habit. This was the incident that transformed him from drug-infused fuck-knuckle who was completely unknown to drug-infused fuck-knuckle who was on the front of every paper.

6. Drummond and Cauty also admitted they hadn't expected the whole Kate Moss drug thing to go as far as it did. 'While we had not planned this, it certainly proved our point,' they said. 'There are many superior artists in the country today, but they never appear in *Heat* or the *Sun*, because they don't have the words "boyfriend of Kate Moss" after their name.' You have to say, they do have a point. And no one had to get covered in sheep's blood this time either.

common by travelling folk, it just didn't all bolt together quite correctly. Bits didn't fit, Drummond and Cauty contradicted themselves in various statements and, more to the point, Pete Doherty denied it all.[7]

More rumor and counter-rumor immediately began to suggest that the admission that it was all a hoax was, in itself, all a hoax, a hoax also perpetrated by the KLF. Another rumor, contrary to that last rumor, suggested that Doherty, Drummond and Cauty were locked in a vicious legal battle over the veracity of the story, which was eventually settled out of court by the discovery of a videotape showing 'Trevor McDermott' singing 'Peggy Sue' at a Butlin's in Devon. Then this latest rumor was rumored to be a hoax and everyone promptly forgot about it.

Who knows what the truth of the hoax is? Or how big the hoax is? Perhaps all of the hoaxing rumored here in these pages is also part of the hoax? In fact, perhaps this whole book is part of the hoax, foisted upon you, the American public, by the KLF, who are using it as a hoax simply to further the original hoax. It's all a hoax within a hoax within a hoax within a hoax within a hoax. Hoax hoax hoax hoax hoax. Isn't it

---

7. But he would, wouldn't he? After all, he was no longer churning out 'That'll Be the Day' to grannies and poor people but instead playing at Live 8 and making a total hash of 'Children of the Revolution' with Elton John.

funny that the more you see the word 'hoax', the more
it loses any meaning and becomes pointless?

Just like Pete Doherty.

Stairway to Hell

❧

There is a story regarding Led Zeppelin that, in much the same way as their song, remains the same whenever you hear it told. It also remains as unpleasant with each telling, but you know me well enough by now to realize that that isn't going to stop me from telling you again. In fact, you may have heard it before on a darkened night and still be suffering flashbacks but here we go. It has to do with ... hmmm ... how shall I put this delicately? Actually I can't[1] so here goes ... it has to do with a large fish and a 17-year-old ginger girl's vagina. There, I've said it.

---

1. I really can't.

The Edgewater Hotel in Seattle was a popular choice for touring bands in the late 60s, not least because you could fish in the sea directly from the window of your room. Led Zeppelin and their terrible entourage checked in in July 1967 to play the Seattle Pop Festival. What happened next and just who was present in the room has been the subject of much discussion over the years. In his book *Hammer of the Gods: The Led Zeppelin Saga*,[2] Stephen Davies describes the incident thus:

A pretty young groupie with red hair was tied to the bed. Led Zeppelin proceeded to stuff pieces of [locally caught] shark into her vagina and rectum.

Classy. It reads like a Jamie Oliver recipe book ghost-written by Satan. But then, in a later book, the finer points of that day's special of Fish Marinated in Groupie are disputed by Richard Cole, the Zeps' ex-tour manager and author of *Stairway to Heaven: Led Zeppelin Uncensored*:[3]

. . . the *true* shark story was that it wasn't even a shark. It was a red snapper and the chick happened to be a fucking redheaded broad with a ginger pussy. And that is the truth.

---

2. New York: William Morrow & Co., 1985, pp. 79–80.

3. New York: HarperCollins, 1992.

She *loved* it. It was like, 'You'd like a bit of fucking, eh? Let's see how *your* red snapper likes *this* red snapper!'

He then goes on to dispute the whole fish/orifice interface, claiming that the story was blown out of all proportion:

[Anyway] it was [just] the *nose* of the fish, and that girl must have come 20 times.

Phew. That's all right then. He also disputes that the whole of Led Zeppelin were involved. According to Cole the experimental fishmongers that day were just drummer John Bonham, the author himself and somebody out of Vanilla Fudge.[4] He goes on to add, eloquently:

That was it. But it was nothing malicious or harmful, no way! No one was *ever* hurt. She might have been hit by a shark a few times for disobeying orders, but she didn't get hurt.[5]

So that clears up that story once and for all. Not all of Led Zeppelin were there but it is true that the wriggling

---

4. The 60s band. Not the ice cream.

5. No word as yet on the medical condition of the fish. If you wait here and there's any change, a vet will come and let you know.

nose of a red snapper became intimately involved with the 'red snapper' of an unnamed 17-year-old girl while she was being hit with a shark.

Just an average day in a rock band.

Jaz Mag

Killing Joke, despite the name, were not really known for their sense of humor. They inspired the likes of Nine Inch Nails and Nirvana and peddled their vision of a doomed world facing a meltdown. These days their frontman, Jaz Coleman, spends his time living on an island 100 miles off the coast of New Zealand in the South Pacific because he's still making plans to survive 'the global eco-industrial apocalypse'[1] that he's seen coming since 1982. Jaz thinks society is about to break

---

1. As revealed in Michael Odell's splendid Jaz Coleman interview in *Q* magazine, July 2006.

down and thus, on his island, he is planning his new social order from underneath the wide brim of a big cowboy hat.

But it wasn't always thus.[2] In those heady days of the 80s when Killing Joke were almost in danger of bothering the charts and mad Jaz[3] was convinced the impending end of mankind was even more impending than he does now, the band had a single to promote. And to do this their record company decided to send a stripper to the offices of a well-known music publication. The stripper, who was of the 'old men gathered in an East End pub in the afternoon' variety, was armed with what was then rather quaintly called a 'ghetto blaster'[4] and she was to play the new Killing Joke single while taking her clothes off.[5]

Trouble was, the record company had reckoned without the 'anti-sexism' vibe that was sweeping the office of the esteemed publication at this time and so, before the stripper had even undone her coat, the

---

2. Actually, it was.

3. I hope Jaz Coleman doesn't read this. He doesn't like reading about things that make him out to be a mental. He once personally dumped a bucket of offal and maggots over the desk of a journalist whose review he didn't like.

4. It would have played 'cassettes', I imagine. Goodness, how old-fashioned.

5. I bet the record company pluggers high-fived and went home early the day they thought of this masterstroke.

intrepid reporting staff all ran away and hid in a different room.[6]

After a while the editor felt a bit sorry for the lady now stripping for herself in an empty office to a soundtrack of industrial punk shouting[7] and went back and begged her to cover up. Switching the tape machine off he then pointed her in the direction of another publication that came out of the same building, a publication he advised would appreciate her charms far more than they. This publication was *Shoot!* magazine, the popular football monthly.[8]

And so the lady clutched her coat about her, picked up her beatbox[9] and made her way next door. Moments later, as the music staff trudged back to their desks, their came a whoopin' and a hollerin' of an appreciative crowd of old men and teenage boys, the likes of which made up the staff of *Shoot!*

The following week *Shoot!*, a magazine that was about

---

6. This was a time, remember, when sexism was being swept aside by that new-fangled 'alternative comedy' and looking at ladies' breasts was now just plain wrong. Benny Hill was now the enemy of the *NME*. Yes, indeed, ladiesangennulmenmynamesbeneltonthangyewandgnight.

7. Once, for the vocals on 1994's *Pandemonium* album, they recorded their industrial punk shouting in the King's Chamber of the Great Pyramid in Egypt. No, really. Told you. Mental.

8. Is it still going? Don't know. I never read it even then. Back in those days I only had eyes for *Buster and Monster Fun* and *The Beezer*.

9. This is not a euphemism.

football, dedicated to football and was football through and through, ran, for one issue only, a music review of the new Killing Joke single. They gave it two stars.

'Chute Me, I'm Only the Piano Player

I feel a 'wicked whisper' coming on. Sssh! Who's the extravagantly gay rock star who once . . . oh fuck it, it's Elton John. Some years ago, before he met His Partner David Furnish™, Elton held a particularly lavish party at his mansion in the Home Counties. Of course the phrase 'Elton' and 'lavish' are made for each other and indeed should they ever split up, doubtless there'll be one almighty courtroom battle as to who gets to keep the wig with a ship in it, but for now, and indeed then, 'Elton' and 'lavish' go hand in hand.

Back to the party. Did I mention it was lavish?

Obviously I don't know exactly what was served[1] but I like to imagine that as Elton received his guests (while lounging on a leopard-shaped day-bed) there were canapés of swan feather and chive, kingfisher and pineapple on sticks, nectar to drink out of crystal slippers and diamond-flavored champagne on tap.[2] Yes, the party was lavish but it was also strictly just for friends of Elton who were also friends of Dorothy.[3]

When it was in full swing[4] and night had well and truly fallen, Elton flicked a discreet switch hidden beneath a table. With an elegant swish the curtains of the ballroom opened to reveal a floodlit lawn descending over several acres toward a glittering, moon-drenched

---

1. I wasn't invited. Possibly on the grounds that I was about five. And I couldn't have gone anyway because Elton's party was on the same day as Lisa Wankling's* and she had cake and balloons and a magician and games and a guinea pig.

2. There may also have been piles of cocaine on silver platters, served to the guest by toga-clad dwarves. On the other hand, most attribute that to Freddie Mercury and, because he's dead and can't sue, I'll attribute that to Freddie Mercury as well. In fact I do, elsewhere in this book.

3. That is, they were in the gayers.

4. I'm not suggesting they were swinging. That is not for me to say.

* She really was called Lisa Wankling and she lived up the road. Sadly I was her friend long before I knew how funny her surname was and sadly, before I realized, we'd lost touch. (Possibly because we soon went to different schools.) Lisa, if you're reading this, drop me a line. I owe you about 25 years of surname mocking.

lake. There were gasps of appreciation from the guests. And then came the distant drone of an airplane. Throwing open the doors Elton led the way outside as the plane got closer and then, as it did, two searchlights lit up to pierce the velvet sky.[5] Their sweeping beam soon picked out the approaching plane flying in quite low over the leafy trees beyond the lake. As their eyes adjusted the guests began to make out the descending shapes of parachutes. Attached to each one was a buff, naked young man.

Did I mention that he was lavish?

---

5. Above Elton's mansion the sky really is made of velvet. He had it specially commissioned in 1975.

Holding Back the Beers

Any tome such as this must contain, possibly by law, at least one mention[1] of the ginger fanny botherer[2] Mick Hucknall and his admirable ability to attract the sort of

---

1. That's handy then, because there are already two other mentions of him (in the unpleasant Faith No More hair dryer story and the one with Sean and Bez out of the Happy Mondays) elsewhere in these pages. Technically then, there are now three mentions of him in this book, which makes it triple complete.

2. Actually, would you believe it but it turns out he's legally not a fanny botherer after all. I apologize. I'd got him all wrong. Turns out then he's a lovely, modest sort of chap. After all, only the most humble, unpretentious, tousle-haired of charmers would once tell the *Observer*: 'I am one of the best singer-songwriters this country has produced. Ever. If people don't like me saying that, tough shit. People should deal with facts. You can't sell 50m albums without something.'*

* Something like a shop, presumably. Or iTunes. Or Amazon at the very least.

beautiful women who are way out of his porky league.[3]
As the lead singer of notable inoffensive elevator music
band Simply Red,[4] Mick has been linked with what the
tabloids like to call a 'string' of women, including
Catherine Zeta Jones, Tracy Shaw, Helena Christensen
and Kathy Lloyd.[5] But none of them were sick all over
him in the back of a taxi.

To her eternal credit, that honor goes to Martine
McCutcheon.[6] In fact it was possibly her finest hour.
It seems that after a Hucknall-arranged romantic date
somewhere in London, perhaps dinner, a premiere or a
dog fight, the canoodling twosome hailed a cab to go
back to Mick's palatial love nest, where, I'm sure, he
was imagining a night of what can only be described
as sexual intercourse would be taking place. What he

---

3. In 2005 he was voted Sky One's number one British Celebrity Minger.
I don't know which is worse, Hucknall, or the fact that Sky One have a
program called *British Celebrity Mingers*.

4. Notable because they're possibly the only band whose other members
remain completely anonymous. Seriously, who the hell are the rest of
Simply Red?

5. How is this possible? I mean it's not like he's got loads of mone . . . Oh,
hang on.

6. You remember. Tiffany off of *EastEnders*. Was in that crap Richard
Curtis film with Hugh Grant.* She had a number one hit with 'This Is My
Moment' in 1999. She once called me a tosser, you know. But at least she
wasn't sick on me.

* Yeah, like that narrows it down. See also 'Wet Wet Dry (Ice)' in this book.

got instead was something a little different. Martine, it seems, had partaken of a little too much of the grape and the grain and was a little more tipsy than he'd perhaps anticipated and so, as the taxi set off back to Palais du Hucknall, the inevitable happened. And it all went in his hair. His lovely, shiny, trademark curly red hair was full of liquid McCutcheon. Hahahahahaha. Haaaaaaaaaaa. Hahahahahahahahahahaha.[7]

Good.

---

7. Hahahahahaha. Haaa. Ha ha. Hahahahahahahahahahaha.

A Fine Time

Now, as we all know, any musician worth his or her salt is just as at home with driving cars into televisions and throwing swimming pools out of hotel bedroom windows as they are with staying up all night and drinking shots of heroin, but I'm not sure that it gets any more rock 'n' roll than this tale of destruction and excess. In fact I don't really know how to write this down. In fact I'm not sure I can. I only hope there are no lawyers reading.[1] Trouble is that the following is such a hedonistic tale of terrible behavior that I just . . . Oh look, I'll just come out and tell you.

Once, backstage at a recording of *Top of the*

---

1. Of course there aren't. They only read large checks or John Grisham.

Pops,[2] Cast smeared crabsticks on Menswear's dressing room door handle.

⋆*Breathes*⋆

I know. It's FUCKING crazy, isn't it? Cast are BONKERS! Armed with the knowledge of all those tales of Keith Moon smashing his hotel room to bits or Ozzy biting a blind mammal's face off, Cast, one Thursday night in 1995, decided to pick up the debauchery torch and run with it because while Menswear were in front of the cameras, they took crabsticks from the green room buffet and wiped them on their rival Britpopians' door! Unbefuckinglievable. Never in all the annals of bad rock 'n' roll behavior has anyone even come close. And that's not the worst of it. Because when Menswear came offstage and went back to their dressing room—the first one of them to open the door GOT FISHY HANDS!!!!!![3] Ahahahahaha!!!!!!

Who says bands these days don't know how to party?[4]

---

2. *Top of the Pops*, or *TOTP* as gits call it, was an institution as British as tea or racism. Launched by shell-suited serial children's hospital botherer Jimmy Savile in 1964 it was the longest-running pop music show on TV. Generation after generation have grown up with it and have then gone on to ask the generation just behind them just what 'this racket is' before adding 'and anyway, you can't hear the words'.

3. Still, this fishy mayhem did in their rivals. Menswear were never seen again while Cast went on to have a Fine Time.

4. I fucking do.

That Man Called Jim Webb Again

Glider boy is back! But this time he's got a shotgun! Nope, that's not the tagline for the latest straight-to-DVD film starring Steven Seagal[1] but a statement that heralds instead the return of everyone's favorite non-engine-winged-wooden-tube pilot.[2]

This time he was in the studio but decided that the snare drum sound he was getting in the control room was too 'spongy' and resolved to do something about it. Much fiddling with microphones and EQ settings

---

1. Everyone's favorite podgy, squinty-faced kickboxer.

2. See 'A Man Called Jim Webb'.

went on but still the drum sound just wasn't as tight or as taut as Jimmy Perfectionist wanted, so after much shouting at the engineers he simply got up, grabbed his coat and left the studio. Not knowing where he'd gone the remaining musicians and engineers continued with the session until, 20 minutes later, Jim came back with a shotgun.

He made them start all over again. Not at gunpoint, you understand, but simply because a sawed-off 12 gauge was how he wanted the snare drum to sound and, as that seemingly couldn't be reproduced with such third-rate old-fashioned things as 'studio equipment' and 'drummers', he solved the problem the only way he knew how. And that way as usual was the way of a madman. As the recording of the song got underway, Shotgun Jim leaned out of the control booth window every few seconds to fire a shot into the air on the beat. The recording took days. Not least because they had to stop every few minutes while he reloaded. Well, that and the fact that, for the sound of the kick drum, he went to fetch a tank.[3]

---

3. I made that up. He didn't. As far as I know.

One-Armed Band Git

You'll be quite aware of course that Rick Allen, the drummer with Def Leppard, has only one arm.[1] We'll take that as read. That's a given. That's yours. You're probably also impressed that he can still play the drums as well as he does with just that one arm, courtesy of a specially adapted drum kit. He is, to date, the only one-armed percussionist in the world who can still make a snare drum emit a sound like a rhino knocking a wall down.[2]

---

1. It fell off during a car accident on New Year's Eve, 1984.

2. Jim Webb, don't get excited. Get away from that zoo.

But that's not the only skill he's learned since becoming one-armed because on July 5, 1995, he was arrested at Los Angeles airport for grabbing his wife Stacy round the neck, threatening to punch her and then dragging her into a toilet and banging her head against the wall. Now let's just think about the logistics of that. First you've gone to the trouble of grabbing your wife around the neck. That uses up one arm. Then, you've followed that up with a threat to punch. That will take another arm which ... oh hang on. Hmmm. Tricky. That means you're going to have to let go of the neck and draw your one remaining fist back in order to facilitate any kind of strike. Trouble is, if you let go of the neck, I'm guessing that the neck's owner isn't going to hang around long enough to suffer the embarrassment of being punched by a monodexter. So you've got a problem. You've issued a threat you can't carry out. So what do you do? OK, utilize what you've got at your disposal by keeping hold of the neck and dragging its owner into a nearby toilet. So far so good. Now what? You still can't punch her because you'd fall over, so what now? Of course! The wall. You can easily bang her head repeatedly against that and the beauty of the plan is that you don't need two limbs to do it. Congratulations! You're a one-armed wifebeater.

Quite rightly the disabled idiot was charged with spousal abuse and ordered to attend Alcoholics Anonymous meetings, receive a year's worth of

bands that sounded like the next one.) It wasn't long, however, before their raw, revivalist rock began to be overshadowed by rumors about their relationship.

With the same jet black hair, pasty skin, and red and white outfits, Jack and Meg Whitestripe had been passing themselves off as brother and sister, the two youngest siblings in a family of ten. Except they were lying. Jack and Meg were in fact ex-husband and wife, having been married in 1996 and divorced in 2000.[3] Which somehow makes their relationship a bit weird. I mean, if you meet someone you are likely to have sex with, at what point do you both like to pretend you're brother and sister? Wedding night? Couple of years later when that sex has become boring and predictable? When you move to Norfolk and you're trying to fit in?[4] Still, the rumors and the slight seediness of the whole thing didn't hurt initial album sales. Everyone lost interest though in 2005 when it was revealed that Jack and Meg were actually in fact just a heavily Botoxed Donny and Marie Osmond who (because of erratic Mormon laws) had been allowed to marry and re-form.[5]

---

3. Jack's real name is John Gillis. He took Meg's name. Presumably on the grounds that 'The Gillis Stripes' sounds shitty. Mind you, that didn't stop The Corrs.

4. Trad. Arr.

5. True.*

* Not true.

Dear Satan . . .

Let's stay awhile and talk Norwegian black metal. Actually, no. Before we get on to the specifics of our Nordic devil-worshipping friends, let us simply mull over the genre of metal known affectionately as 'black'.

Black metal is described by various encyclopedias as 'a very specific form of music that must adhere to a particular metal "sub-genre style" in order for it to be a part of the genre within which the lyrical and philosophical/political ideology of the music takes more precedence in defining the genre itself'. To the rest of us, however, it's just some blokes dressing up and jumping about while shouting.[1] And in that respect it's not a million miles away from, say, *Aladdin* at the Orchard Theatre in Dartford. Proponents of the former include Darkthrone, Enslaved and Mercyful Fate, while proponents of the latter include Cannon and Ball and, with the painful inevitability of some sort of incurable cancer, someone out of *Neighbours*.

But while, to most, death metal is naught but a pantomime, I have to report that the Norwegians take it a whole lot more seriously. Since 1992 in the land of fjords and moose[2] more than 60 church fires have been blamed on the black metal scene,[3] not to mention countless cases of aforementioned moose[4] being

---

1. You see, heavy metal is joyfully unique in that its proponents like to outdo each other in an increasingly absurd and pointless fashion. First, apparently, there was heavy metal then soft metal. Then came black metal then death metal then heavy metal again then doom metal then folk metal then glam metal then gothic metal then grindcore then industrial metal then metalcore then neoclassical metal then nu-metal then power metal then progressive metal then symphonic metal then thrash metal then speed metal then alt metal then avant-garde metal then Celtic metal then Christian metal then classic metal then dark metal then epic metal then extreme metal then the new wave of British heavy metal then rapcore then stoner metal then Viking metal then heavy metal for a third time and so on and so forth. Oh for heaven's sake, grow up.

2. Moose? Mooses? Meece?

3. Not the worst nor most demeaning act of a Norwegian black metal band by any means. For instance, in 2006 one of them, Lordi (who dress as monsters), won the Eurovision Song Contest. Christ, that's sick.

4. Moose? Mooses? Meece?

pushed into equally aforementioned fjords.[5] And it's somewhere round about here that Mayhem come in. Brilliantly, genuinely, just to prove how hard and 'metal' he was, much metaller, in fact, than his metal peers, Mayhem's lead singer, Dead,[6] simply committed suicide. So what, I hear you say. Lots of people commit suicide. Ted Moult[7] for one and he wasn't particularly metal. Fair enough, you have a point. But concentrate because here comes the metal bit. Dead's bandmate, the lead guitarist Euronymous,[8] then ate his brain.

Naturally this was just about the hardest and most metallist thing that had ever been done on the Norwegian black metal circuit. This really did put the burning of churches into perspective. Any old Satan worshipper can set fire to a chapel but eating a suicidal black metal singer's brain? Different league, mate. Top that. All right then. Just as Mayhem's metal crown looked like a, ahem, 'Dead' cert, along came

---

5. Not really. I made that bit up.

6. That's right. His name was 'Dead'. He was called 'Dead'. How black metal is that? His real name of course was probably Colin.

7. Ted Moult was the TV face and voice of Everest double glazing. He used to advertise said glass by being filmed (from inside a lounge) standing outside some patio doors and switching a wind machine on in order to demonstrate its soundproofing qualities. Sadly, he later committed suicide by shooting himself at home. I'm not sure this was part of the campaign, although his neighbors later said they hadn't heard a thing.

8. Real name probably Simon.

the member of a rival band who simply killed Mr. Euronymous on the grounds that he had a more evil reputation.

Let's recap. Lead singer kills himself, brain is eaten by fellow band member, brain eater is killed by rival. Thus he wins.

And from all this we can conclude then that the rules of black metal are only slightly less forbidding than those of cricket.

Curiosity Time

Ben Volpeliere-Pierrot. Not a name to try to rattle your lager-boozed tongue around after four pints of anything remotely beer-flavored. Actually, to be honest, it's not really the sort of name you should attempt to rattle your tongue around ever. Ever. I've just written it down and I still don't know how to pronounce it properly. No one does. It's like 'schedule' or 'tomato' if you're an American.[1] But, on the plus side, you probably won't

---

1. They say 'to*may*to', we say 'tomato'. We say 'potato', they say 'pot*ar*to'. We say 'There's a problem with child obesity', they say 'Fuck the vegetables,* pass me another bucket of fizzy lardcorn. And is anyone having that last Twinkie?'**

* Yes, I do know that a tomato is technically a fruit. Stop writing in.

** I don't even know what a Twinkie is.

ever *have* to conjure with his moniker because his beret-topped face has long since vanished from pop's proud pantheon.

Back in 1987, though, Ben and his band, Curiosity Killed the Cat, were supping at the cream of pop's milky teat but, like so many bands before and since, they soon found that pop's fickle hand[2] would only allow them to feed for so long. That's why just after their initial 15 minutes of f(l)ame had burned out, they often found themselves as the 'irony' booking at many a student union gig and it was from one such event in Southampton in the early 90s that this tale doth stem.

The place was packed. These student gigs often are. After all, who doesn't like dancing to the cheesy hits of the bands of yesteryear? With the possible exception of Goths? But, for those of us who don't wear black lipstick round our eyes and enjoy a nice hobby of self-harming, what could be better than an evening of the 80s?[3] And so it was that Curiosity were rattling through their hit[4] and, perhaps carried away with the moment,

---

2. The hand that was presumably squeezing the teat. I may be taking this metaphor too far. And it's not even really a metaphor.

3. Actually, probably loads of things: a cold beer on a summer's day, a *West Wing* box set, the untimely demise of Justin Lee Collins in some kind of machine, to name but three.

4. 'Misfit', probably. Although they did have 'Straight Back Down to Earth' as well.

Ben Volauvent-Pencil decided to hold the microphone out into the crowd like a proper rock star might and implore the irony moshers[5] down the front to sing. It was only after he was satisfied that his audience still knew every word of the chorus of 'Misfit' ten years on that Ben retracted his arm from the student mob. And it was then that he discovered that someone had nicked his watch.

Yes, while his hand was held out into the crowd to enhance their 80s experience with a gesture of bereted pop solidarity, some student had had it away with his Timex. He stopped the gig mid-song. 'Someone has nicked my watch,' he said. 'If I don't get it back right now we're not playing any more and getting off.'

He never saw it again.

---

5. Can you 'mosh' to Curiosity? On balance, probably not.

Born to Canoe

Born and raised in Noo Joisey under an industrial sky to the clang of steelmills and the sweet stench of hard graft, Bruce Springsteen is the champion of the working man. Which is why it comes as something of a surprise to learn that he once became embroiled in a court battle with two of his own roadies because they broke his canoe.

In 1985 Springsteen's Glory Days were upon him.[1]

---

1. It was well before the miserable *Ghost of Toad Hall* album or whatever it was called or that dirgy thing about the World Trade Center. I mean, come on, Bruce . . . where's the new 'Thunder Road'? *Born to Run*? Even the one on *Born in the USA* that seems to be about a mechanic cum kiddy fiddler was better than your recent output. Yawn. Listen up, introspective rockers of America, and listen good. Yes, 9/11 happened. We get it. Get over it.

The biggest album in the world was *Born in the USA* and it even had a picture of his arse on the cover. He was filling stadium after stadium with his fist-waving patrio-rock and the sight of people waving the American flag with its gaudy arrangement of stars and stripes was, thanks to Bruce, nowhere near as nauseating as it usually is.

But like any rock star on the road at the helm of a metaphorical and literal juggernaut Bruce wanted his home comforts, and to relax between gigs he liked nothing more than tripping the local waterways fantastic in his canoe. The rural backwaters of the US were a haven away from the rigors of pompous guitar-driven country rock and anthemic opuses of growing up and/or longing to escape from a dead-end job, and it is not hard to imagine the tiny figure of Bruce, tearing the sleeves off yet another of his denim jackets and setting himself adrift on peaceful, relaxing waters.[2]

Which is why, to look after his canoe and transport it safely between venues, he employed two canoe roadies. Canoe roadieing is a highly specialized job which involves years of training and demands the very best from the dedicated professionals who practice its

---

2. Perhaps on 'The River'? Although, according to that song, for his birthday he got a union card and a wedding coat. No mention whatsoever of a canoe.

rare art. There's also no such thing, which is why he entrusted his pride and joy to a couple of hairy-arsed flightcase humpers instead. All very well and good until one day the roadies decided to transport the canoe to the next gig by paddling it there. No protective packaging or trucks for this mother, oh no. A quick glance at a map showed the intrepid pair that careful navigation of a waterway would get them almost directly from one venue to the next and, believing that such a journey would be a break from the rigors of the road, they set off to bask in some of Bruce's reflected relaxation technique.

Unfortunately for them they were shit at canoeing so they sank it.

It gets a bit confused at this point. Some say Bruce took them to court and sued them for canoe loss. Others say he just docked their pay. Some (admittedly half-hearted and lazy) research indicates that the roadies quit and sued Bruce for $6 million in punitive damages, citing the docked pay and unpaid overtime. To be honest, if all Bruce did was dock their pay I reckon they got off lightly. You don't lose a man's canoe and not have to suffer some kind of retribution. Still, however it came about, the battle ended up in the courtroom, where The Boss found himself instead becoming The Man and suddenly for the next six years instead of 'Dancing in the Dark' he was arguing the toss over a canoe. That's right, for *six* years.

Six years of canoe-based litigation. And then it was eventually settled out of court.

I'd like to think such an experience could help explain why he was so obviously in a bad mood when he wrote 'Streets of Philadelphia', but it doesn't.

'Leave It, Omar, He's a Raspberry'

Welcome to the Casino, ladies and gentlemen. Now place your bets as we see where Omar Sharif's fist lands. Congratulations, if you bet on Ian Dury's face, you're a winner.

Come with me into the plush velvety surroundings of a casino in West London. Inside, the handsome, suave, debonair and *Magnum PI*–style mustachioed[1] film star Omar Sharif is at the roulette table. He's a casino

---

1. A great big bushy thing. The sort that hangs down over the upper lip like a hair equivalent of those hanging bead things that local newsagents have to keep flies out of the back room.

regular, and an expert bridge player, but that's not all he's good at because he's also fairly skilled at punching people in the face.

From actors (reportedly he hit John Noble[2] with a table lamp in India, 2004[3]) and policemen (headbutted one in a casino, 2003[4]) to valet parking attendants (complaint filed by one who accused him of assault and racial abuse, 2005[5]), you'd think Omar's reputation when it came to the gaming tables would have preceded him. But I guess if you're Ian Dury—cult punk poet extraordinaire and polio sufferer—then you know no fear. As our hero passed Omar he nodded and acknowledged the fiery hirsute one just as he was laying a bet.

With a great bellow of angry rage Sharif leapt at the Blockheads' lead singer and they fell to the ground in a punching fury of shattering whiskey glasses, casino chips, moustaches and crutches. It was then that a

---

2. Played a baddie in *Lord of the Rings: The Return of the King*. Apparently.

3. According to the *Daily Mirror*, November 2004. They were in India filming *One Night with the King*. Apparently.

4. This was in Paris. He was convicted, fined and got a suspended sentence. And Omar's reaction? 'It made me the hero of the whole of France. To headbutt a cop is the dream of every Frenchman.' Encore!

5. According to records of the Los Angeles Superior Court. It should be noted that Omar pleaded not guilty and was eventually cleared of the charges.

single, solitary cry rent the air. Over the sound of the flying fists came the cry of the Blockheads' drummer sounding for all the world like an anxious girlfriend caught up in a pub scrap. For those that were there it was a sentence that must haunt them to this day. For the rest of us it is a phrase that should be immortalized on Dury's premature gravestone:

'Leave it, Omar, he's a raspberry.'[6]

Let's hear that again:

'Leave it, Omar, he's a raspberry.'

It's almost poetic. I can't think why drummers are never allowed to write any songs.[7]

---

6. It's rhyming slang as used by cock-er-neys who want to appear stereotypical. Raspberry ripple = Cripple. There is no record as to whether Omar understood it.

7. Phil Collins, are you listening?

Where Eagles Fear to Tread

Driving across the Nevada desert late one night a few years ago, myself and my friend Alan were weary. We'd been out all day, driving out of Las Vegas at dawn to get to Area 51[1] before, circling round the top of the Nellis Air Force Base in Nevada, we'd driven back to Vegas via a quick blast through California's Death Valley, and then, with darkness falling, we crossed back over the border and headed down to Vegas. It was a long day of road tripping, memorable for many reasons, but not least for the moment when we crested a low hill in our

---

1. The nonexistent US military base that pretends not to be there. Even though it's on Google Earth and, thanks to our trip across an unmarked road in an unmarked bit of desert, I've seen it with my very own eyes. Well, up until some unmarked men in an unmarked jeep wearing unmarked sunglasses carrying unmarked automatic weapons made it quite clear we should go away. We went away.

open-topped car at about 11 p.m. and saw the bright lights of Vegas burning in the black distance about 60 miles away. We were literally on a dark desert highway, cool wind in our hair. And it was at that moment that the Lord Jesus did smile on us and he did make the Eagles' 'Hotel California' come on the radio.[2]

It was perfect. The perfect band with the perfect song for a perfect moment in time as we cruised along above the sand and beneath the stars. But while there's plenty of room at the Hotel California,[3] there certainly isn't much onstage when the Eagles hit town.

---

2. Of course he didn't. Even assuming the Lord Jesus was real and not made up like the Abominable Snowman or Bono, then to accept this premise we'd somehow have to consider the possibility that He'd chosen to mark His second coming not by walking on the sick or turning water into loaves (or whatever David Blaine–style thing He was planning to wow mankind with) but instead by assuming financial and creative control of a tiny country rock music station on the California/Nevada border. And then, out of the countless Dixie Chicks and/or Shania Twain tracks He *could've* played He'd chosen, at that moment, especially for two dusty men in a car, to spin the correct Eagles song. It's all a bit far-fetched if you ask me. Although that never bothered Dan Brown. ★*Scribbles idea for new* Da Vinci Code–*style book on back of envelope.*★

3. And still no one knows what this is about. The Devil has been suggested, as have drugs and a whorehouse. For me the line 'you can check out any time you like but you can never leave' seems to be the pivotal moment of the song. It conjures up a sense of crushing despair and the notion that such a suicidal mindset may well remain with you wherever you go. You can never quite wash the experience from your mind, it will always be there haunting you and creeping into your darkest dreams. For this reason I think it's about a Travelodge.

Yes, these days Glenn Frey, Don Henley, Joe Walsh and the other one(s) apparently do not get on well at all. On tour to promote their last studio album the band was a mess of acrimony, infighting and the sort of personality differences that only an arrest for possessing cocaine, quaaludes,[4] and marijuana after a nude underage prostitute had drug-related seizures in a hotel room can bring.[5] In addition, Glenn Frey and Don Felder had to be separated by police and fellow band members backstage at a 1980 fund-raising concert. Then, brilliantly, on the last night of the tour on July 31st in Long Beach, California, it all went off like a Muslim rucksack.

Tempers boiled and, as the show progressed, Frey and Felder spent the entire show describing to each other the beating each planned to give the other backstage just as soon as the gig was over.[6] As soon as

---

4. Quaalude. I love the word 'quaalude'. I don't even know what one is but it's great because it sounds like a futuristic space drug from space. It's a great word. Roll it around your tongue and it becomes the sort of mad noise that even Jeff Wayne would have balked at while recording *The War of the Worlds*.

5. That was Don Henley that was. He was charged with 'contributing to the delinquency of a minor'.

6. How cool is that? It's like when you're in a math lesson and someone threatens to 'get you' after school outside the gates. 'Only three more songs until I kick your ass, pal,' Frey recalls Felder telling him near the end of the band's set.

it was Frey launched an assault on Felder, who protected himself with his guitar. Within seconds, the rest of the band had joined in. It took a dozen roadies to pull the warring factions apart.[7]

Funnily enough the Eagles then disbanded vowing, quite categorically, never ever ever ever *ever* to share the same stage again. They went their separate ways; Glenn Frey recorded 'The Heat Is On' and Don Henley dabbled with the 'Boys of Summer'.[8] But later their artistic integrity[9] demanded that they re-form for the fans[10] and so in 1994 they shambled back onstage for the first of about 20 annual farewell tours. But wait. Hadn't they sworn never to do this? Hadn't they expressed such hatred for each other that the idea of any sort of reunion was preposterous? Surely this was hypocritical? After all the bitter fighting with each other hadn't they sworn blind that they would never, under any circumstances play together on the same stage again? Yes, but that's fine because they'd come up with an idea that solved this problem entirely. And it was called 'carpet'.

Yes, since then, whenever the Eagles play together

---

7. Source: http://www.eaglesfans.com/info/articles/old_devils.htm

8. And was subsequently charged with 'contributing to the delinquency of the boys of summer'.

9. Or 'money'.

10. Or for money.

onstage they each stand on a separate square of different-colored carpet, which ensures that technically, yes, they never actually play together on the same 'stage'. They're quite happy playing together on offcuts from World of Rugs it seems, but certainly not on the same stage, no siree. This, I imagine they believe, doesn't compromise their artistic integrity, with the bonus that the resulting buildup of static means that they can do wonders with balloons at children's parties.

Private Dancer

It's the Year of Our Lord 1989 and after an eight-year sabbatical the Rolling Stones set off around the globe on their record-breaking Steel Wheels Tour, a tour that took in oh, I dunno, loads of dates and venues[1] and was the first of their by now familiar ultra-budget, big-lipped assaults on stadiums worldwide. It also reunited

---

1. I would have filled in the details here but made the mistake of relying on my friend Nick Bosworth. He's the biggest Rolling Stones fan you can imagine so I called him and asked him for the technical details of the Steel Wheels Tour. Needless to say, by the time my deadline rolled around, he still hadn't gotten back to me. Thus I am making it publicly known here in these pages that he's a twat.

Jagger and Richards, their feuds and rows of the 80s put aside as they set off in big trucks full of lights and sound and staging.

The rig for this was huge. Tons of metal, dozens of stuff and positively loads of other big, heavy concerty things.[2] Anyway, the point is that it was spectacular and the Stones camp was certain that fans everywhere were going to be blown away. Except for one small sour-faced fly in the ointment that went by the name of Bill Wyman.[3] Wyman was of course the Stones' bass player and, significantly, *Steel Wheels* was to be his last studio album with the band. He officially quit in January 1993. On this tour, then, he wore a face not dissimilar to an arse that had not just been quite liberally and energetically smacked, but that had also had a foreign object put up it.

It wasn't long, then, as he went through the musical motions, before his craggy, humorless features began to get on the rest of the band's nerves. They'd spent millions on this tour; it was supposed to be their joyous comeback and, as critics continued to point to their combined age being somewhere in the region of 875, they needed to look like they were enjoying it. They wanted to look like they were having fun performing in this circus we call rock 'n' roll and not, during their

---

2. Ditto. In fact he's a double twat.

3. Si si il est un rock star les miserables.

big side-of-stage screen closeup, look instead like they were suffering from an attack of Wyman's Hemorrhoidal Gout.[4] They needed Bill to lighten up. What they needed was a plan.

In the end it was the staging that came to the rescue, the answer being a simple one designed specifically to appeal to the foibles of Wyman. In front of his bass position stage left, roadies and technical crew were instructed to cut a big circular hole to the understage area below. In the hole, way out of view of anyone in the audience yet directly in Bill's line of sight, a small podium was constructed. On this podium, every night, at every gig, in every city on the worldwide Steel Wheels Tour, a young naked girl would be paid to dance in an effort to cheer up old misery guts.[5] It worked. Apparently he smiled twice.

---

4. This may not be an actual condition. Don't trust me, I'm not a doctor.

5. Bill 'favors' ladies at the lower end of the age spectrum. I draw the judge's attention to his famous relationship, at the age of 47, with the then 13-year-old Mandy Smith. And the fact that not long ago, in the reception area of a London radio station, I saw him make a valiant attempt to get into the knickers of the 17-year-old receptionist. She didn't have a clue who he was and I rejoiced when, after she'd watched his caretakers take him away, she turned to her colleague to say: 'Wot was 'e like, eh? As if I'd shag some old homeless bloke.'

Honestly, Pop Stars Today . . .

Billie Piper is now an actress of course, her big break arriving in 2005 in the shape of Rose, the glamorous, buck-toothed assistant in the remake of *Doctor Who*. But before that she was a pop star with up to one hit to her name,[1] and it was during this hit that she found herself on the bill of a Capital Radio Party in the Park sort of tour[2] with the likes of Atomic Kitten and Westlife and their unholy, pointless ilk.[3]

---

1. Or was it two? Hang on. I'll look . . . Blimey. It's actually *eight* Top 40 hits. And three number ones. Thank you, messrs. Gambaccini, Rice and Rice.

2. Capital Radio's Party in the Park–type tours were, if you can imagine such a nightmare, the aural and visual equivalent of the plague, fanning out

At this time little Billie Piper must have been about eight or something and was going out with Ritchie out of 5ive.[4] She had her mum as a chaperone—bless—and was sharing the entire floor of a hotel with the rest of the 5ive, the Kitten and the Life. Now, when bands are in hotels we all know what happens. There's often destruction on a massive scale. Such events are well catalogued, some even discussed in this book.[5] But give an entire floor to four or 5ive bands consisting of children and what do you think happens? That's right, an enormous pillow fight.

---

across the country spreading their lightweight pop germs into the eyes and ears of 12-year-olds. It was basically a record company con trick, as for every five mimed Westlife songs you also got at least three mimed Phixx tracks and some bollocks by 'A1'. Whatever they are. Capital Radio would then slap their name on it, fill the gaps with trite fuckwits, or 'DJs' as they insist on calling them, and the whole sorry lot would rock up in your home-town. To my shame I was actually one of those trite fuckwits once. It was at 'Power in Portsmouth'. I had to introduce Adam Rickett. I'm so sorry. I was young and I needed the money.

3. Actually, come to think of it, it may have been the Smash Hits Poll Winners Party but you get the gist. The point is, despite them both having the word 'party' in the title they're about as far removed from a party as you can get. Not unless your idea of a party is a hate-filled room where 10,000 12-year-olds are shrieking into their fizzy pop. I tell you, unless you're Jonathan King, that's no party.

4. That's how they wrote it. 5ive. They were called 'Five' (there were five of them) and they spelt it '5ive'. 5ucking 6unts.

5. For instance, when Led Zeppelin ran amok in hotel corridors they did it with motorbikes. Not pillows, *motorbikes*.

That's it. That's how rock 'n' roll they all were. They had a pillow fight. OK, it was in the corridors, but still. You'd think, wouldn't you, that they could've come up with something a bit better than that! Kids these days are right little bastards when they want to be and these kids are in *bands* for goodness' sake. They could've at least put hoodies on and nipped out to go shoplifting or something. But no, pillow fighting. You'd hope that Ritchie out of 5ive would have been at least trying to get a hand in Billie's knickers on the stairwell, wouldn't you?[6] But no. Nothing. Nada. Naught. Apart from pillows.

Right. Come on, kids of today. Think of this story as a warning, a clarion call to arms. A plea from me to you. There you are all wanting to be in *X-Factor*–style bands, singing close harmony pop from atop stools for some toddlers but come on, what's that doing for the future of bad boy behavior? The last one of your kind to do anything interesting was Cheryl Tweedy out of Girls Aloud[7] so come on, get out there and burn something down. Next time you're playing one of these sorts of things and you're introduced by June Sarpong on a beach in Weston-super-Mare punch her in the face. Cheryl Tweedy would. When Vernon Kay or

---

6. After all, there was that story about her when she . . . [This bit omitted for legal reasons].

7. See 'Girls Aloud Fought the Law and the Law Won'.

even, God forbid, Neil Fox brings you onstage at something, calmly, and in full view of the crowd, piss up his legs. And next time you see Fearne Cotton, kick her in the balls.

Pillow fighting my arse. Come on, bands! You owe it to your legacy.

Dude (Looks Like a Cokehead)

Long before they found 'Love in an Elevator' or Steven Tyler accompanied Ben Affleck's tongue as it wormed its way into his own daughter's mouth,[1] Aerosmith were *the* drug-straddling rock band that have now become the byword for a drug-straddling rock band.[2] Their intake of the rock 'n' roll lifestyle, be it in bottle

---

1. In the 1998 movie *Armageddon*, to the strains of her own father singing 'I Don't Want to Miss a Thing', Liv Tyler shags Ben Affleck. This is faintly disturbing and wrong. Not the fact that it's her dad you understand, just the idea that anyone would want to shag Ben Affleck.

2. Other bywords for drug-straddling rock bands include Motley Crüe, Guns n' Roses and Marti Pellow.

or powder form, was the stuff of folklore, leaving many people to wonder even now just exactly why they aren't dead.

In the mid-70s this five-piece juggernaut of messy music embarked on a coast-to-coast tour of the United States, leaving more and more of their addled minds behind as they rode from town to town. By the end, they were a liability and even their own livers had almost given up supporting them in concert, let alone anyone else. 'Twas then that they arrived back in Ohio, six months after they'd played it at the start of the tour. During 'rehearsals',[3] their tour manager suggested that, as they'd been playing the same set day in, day out for half a year and considering they'd played this venue on the tour before, they should vary the order of the songs and perhaps even open with what was normally their big encore, 'Walk This Way',[4] by way of a change.

Through eyes the color and consistency of death the band mumbled something in the affirmative. The hour approacheth, the venue filleth and gay-looking flowery

---

3. Who knows what form these so-called rehearsals took by this stage. Probably just involved Steven Tyler lying in a pool of his own speedball vomit wearing only a gay scarf.

4. 'Walk This Way' was covered by Girls Aloud (them again) and the Sugababes for Comic Relief 2007. I expect terminally ill children and the desperate population of the urban slums of Ghana were, like, well impressed: 'Wow. Girls Aloud, you say? Fuck me, I might just try and stay alive long enough to download their next album.'

scarves were duly tied-eth to mic stands by roadies. The houselights dimmed, the stage lights picked out messrs. Tyler, Perry, Hamilton, Kramer and Whitford, and they staggered onstage to open the show with what was normally their big closer.

'Waaaaalllkkkk thissss waaaaaaaaaay!' screeched Tyler through his trademark leather lips. 'Taaaaaaaaaaaaaalk thissss waaaaaaaaaaay!' the crowd screeched back, delirious that the big hit was first. 'Waaaaalk this waaaaaaaaaay!' screeched Tyler again as the crowd went crazy-ass crazy. And so it went on to the end. Eventually their first song grew to its shuddering climax.[5] And finished. The final chord was deafening, the band were triumphant and the crowd went crazy-ass crazier. And that was when a mashed-up Aerosmith, thinking they'd just finished the whole gig, left the stage and went home.

Thank you, Ohio, and goodnight.[6]

---

5. Uurgh. Reminds me of Tyler and Affleck again. Now I just feel sick.

6. It should be noted of course that Joe Perry has long since claimed that this never happened. 'For a start,' he says, (and I'm paraphrasing) 'it was "Dream On" not "Walk This Way" and we weren't so mashed that we walked off after we'd played it, it was just that we were so mashed we played it twice by accident.' Oh, that's all right then. Thanks, Joe.

Fall from Grace

The Fall's charismatic[1] frontman and lyricist Mark E. Smith was always a bit of a scatterbrain.[2] Long championed by John Peel on Radio 1, the erudite[3] Mr. Smith once appeared on BBC2's *Newsnight* program to be interviewed following Peel's untimely death in 2004.[4] The presenter, Gavin Esler, was fighting a losing battle as Mark, in the Manchester studio, seemed to be leaning dangerously close to the camera lens with his

---

1. Mental.

2. Mental.

3. Mental.

4. *Newsnight* interview, Tuesday, October 26, 2004. Conducted by Gavin 'He's no Paxman, is he?' Esler.

tongue lolling in and out like a lizard with Down's syndrome. The conversation went a bit like this:

Gavin Esler: Mark . . .

(Mark is exploring his own mouth)

Gavin Esler: Mark, that is amazing just to listen to that, er, tribute to [John Peel] there from . . .

(Mark is jabbering indistinctly)

Gavin Esler: . . . er . . . that everybody, from T-Rex onwards, every generation seemed to find, or he seemed to find something for every generation, including The Fall.

(Silence)

Mark: . . . Er, am I allowed to speak now?

Presenter: Yes, go ahead . . .

Mark: Er, right *(chuckles[5])*, er, er, yeah, whatever, whatever you say. *(Looks a bit puzzled)*

Presenter: Erm . . .

---

5. To be honest, it may have been another jabber.

Mark: Eh? Are you the new one? Are you the new DJ?

(Smiles. Does the mouth/tongue/exploring/jabber thing)

Interviews, you see, don't come easy for Mr. E. Smith. Indeed, back in the heady days of the late 80s, one journalist settled down to record his wise words for a piece in a music paper. Mark immediately picked up the heroic hack's dictation machine and marveled at its compact size and portability, remarking that such a device would be useful for recording song lyrics on the road but expressing some concern about the availability of the tiny tapes that were its recording lifeblood. The journalist began to reassure the great Mancunian[6] poet as to their ubiquity but was stopped in his tracks by a characteristic tongue loll: 'I went into an electrical shop to get one,' jabbered Mark. 'And the bloke told me exactly the same.'

'Of course he did,' replied the journalist. 'This is the future of audio technology.'[7]

---

6. Mental.

7. Yeah. iPod Schmipod.*

* The iPod Schmipod is due for release by Apple in 2012. Unless of course it's 2012 now and you're reading this having found it in the remainder bin in a Works Publishers outlet on the moon. In which case there's every chance that the iPod Schmipod never got past the ideas stage, the market for anti-Semitic MP3 players having bottomed out somewhere around mid-2009.

'I told the bloke "Bollocks",' replied Mark. 'I said to him: "These tapes are bollocks and they're impossible to get."'

It seems the shopkeeper, doubtless anxious to make a sale, argued the point. 'Difficult to get? It's 1989,[8] mate. You can get these tapes in record shops, hardware shops, newsagents, anywhere. In fact, these microcassettes are going to be *the* recording medium of the 90s and beyond.'[9]

'So I said to him,' continued Mark, '"in that case I'll take the machine and ten cassettes."'

'Sorry,' says the shopkeeper. 'We haven't got any.'

---

8. The year of the Jive Bunny and The Mastermixers. Ah, 1989, how you spoiled us.

9. Duh. *Makes spaz noise*

You Give Accountancy a
Bad Name

In 1986/87 Bon Jovi were no longer livin' on a prayer and were instead livin' on a lifestyle of private planes, stadiums and hair that had been specially shipped in from a barber's worst nightmare. Their album *Slippery When Wet* had gone enormous and they'd just broken through to a new audience of soft rockers with their sing-along anthems about giving love a bad name and songs about Tommy and Gina.[1] And it was at the

---

1. Tommy and Gina, you will recall, were the heroes of 'Livin' on a Prayer'. Gina, it transpired, worked the diner all day, workin' for her man (that was Tommy), to bring home her pay. Tommy, for his part, used to work on the docks, but since the union's 'bin' on strike he appears to have done fuck all. Lazy bastard.

height of this late-80s success that Jon Bon Jovi, being a benevolent sort of soul, decided that he would give a leg up, a helping hand if you will, to another band who were struggling, as they themselves had for many years, to break through to the mainstream.

And so he picked Skid Row.[2] Jon BJ had been a friend of Skid Row guitarist Dave 'The Snake' Sabo[3] for a while and was now in a position to help them to secure a record deal. But he'd reckoned without Skid Row's lead singer, Sebastian Bach.[4] Record deal duly secured, Skid Row's initial flame burned brightly with 'I Remember You', 'Youth Gone Wild' and '18 and Life'

---

2. Skid Row, like Bon Jovi, hailed from New Jersey and had a similar taste in poncing about like big girls.

3. Excellent. It's great when guitarists have a middle name like this. I'm presuming that Dave 'The Snake' Sabo had a snake. I base this theory on the fact that Tony 'The Hat' Clarkin, the guitarist with Magnum, was so called because he had a hat. It's the one thing that guitarists have in common with East End criminals of the 60s. For instance Jack 'The Hat' McVitie was so called because he also had a hat and Ronnie 'Sex with Men' Kray was called that because he had sex with men. It's a simple but effective system.

4. He was an unruly fellow. There was what is often referred to as 'The Bottle Incident'. Opening for Aerosmith in 1989, Bach was hit by a bottle, which he promptly threw back into the crowd where it hit a girl in the face. And then he leapt into the crowd to beat up the person who originally threw it at him. Then he got back onstage to finish the show. To say the crowd has somewhat turned against him by this point would be an understatement. And then, when they came off, Bach was arrested and tried on charges of assault and battery. Oh and once, for a photo shoot, he wore a T-shirt that said 'Aids Kills Fags Dead'.

all charting on both sides of the Atlantic. But then Sebastian accused Jon Bon Jovi of ripping them off.

The essence of his claim was that JBJ had not only seen a million faces and rocked them all but had also seen a million dollars or so of earnings which, even though he'd given them a significant leg up rock's Lycra ladder, our Seb thought would be better off in the pocket of *his* leopard-print spandex leggings. Understandably this led to rock tension, the most joyous moment of which came just as Bon Jovi were going onstage at a huge outdoor stadium gig in the States. Skid Row were supporting and had already been on. There was the usual half-hour or so turnaround while Bon Jovi's equipment[5] was set up and then it was show-time. The band, one by one, took to the stage. Tico Torres (drummer) first, then Alec John Such (bass),[6] then Dave Bryan (keyboards), followed closely by Richie Sambora (guitar). And then Jon Bon Jovi, all sunglasses, hair and expensive teeth, made to run up the stage ramp. It was at this point that Sebastian Bach decided to quiz the rock god frontman over what he

---

5. I like to think this included 3 × Beds of Roses, 5 × bottles of Bad Medicine and at least 1 × Cowboy on a Steel Horse.

6. He's not with them anymore. It's Hugh McDonald now, in case you're interested.*

* Oh, you're not. Even so, I should add at this point that, with no trace of irony whatsoever, I actually do ♥ Bon Jovi. I think they rock. And I know all the words to all their songs. Please don't hate me.

considered to be financial irregularities in the band's last set of accounts. He was particularly concerned with the figures concerning income and the fiscal abnormalities that his personal audit of the record royalty balance sheet had thrown up. As he ran past Bach, without even breaking stride, slowing down or even glancing in his direction, Jon Bon Jovi simply punched him in the face and moments later was in front of 100,000 fans, well into the first verse of, somewhat appropriately, 'Lay Your Hands on Me'.

I'm not sure they've spoken since.

Pavarotti Goes to the Toilet

Pavarotti, the fat singer, contractually had to be no farther than 50 meters from a toilet at any time—including onstage, where a special double-size disabled portaloo had to be installed behind the percussion section.[1]

If he strayed more than 50 meters from a toilet at any time, Pavarotti simply exploded.[2]

That's it.

---

1. The man who built Pavarotti's stage told me this yesterday. Thus it is true.

2. Like the bomb on the bus in *Speed*. Or Rutger Hauer's head in *Wedlock*. Out of all the stories in this book, this one is the one that is a *fact*.

Queen Elton of John

Where were you on that fateful day? The terrible morning in August 1997 when the world woke up to the awful, awful news that Elton John was going to sing at Princess Diana's funeral?

She was the nation's Queen of Doe-y eyes and Royal Custodian of George Michael's 80s Haircut, and when she exited this life on the losing side of a pillar fight, the world went into mourning. And none more so than her good friend Sir Elton John, who immediately knew he just had to pay a special tribute to his fag-hag land-mine friend. And so it came to pass that he phoned his longtime songwriting partner, Bernie Taupin, in Los Angeles.

'Bernie,' he sobbed through wet-with-tears strands of his great big wig with a ship in it.[1] 'I need to sing a tribute to Diana at her funeral. Something along the lines of "Candle in the Wind".'

Thus, just one day before the funeral Bernie faxed Elton a rewrite of his classic song[2] and, as is befitting our famously short-fused, piano-playing national treasure, Sir Elton went ballistic.

Sadly, due to a bad connection on their transatlantic line, Bernie had slightly misheard what Elton had said. What Elton had actually asked for was a new song about Diana 'written in the *style* of "Candle in the Wind"', i.e., a soppy ballad. What Bernie had done was simply change the lyrics to the old Marilyn Monroe song, chucking something down about 'England's Rose' and 'smuggling soldiers into Kensington Palace for sex'.[3] Elton was massive with fury, but now it was too late. The funeral was tomorrow and there was no time. Our colorful friend, tiaras by now firmly out of

---

1. See also ''Chute Me, I'm Only the Piano Player'.

2. Originally written about Marilyn Monroe of course, in 1973. Included the lines about the young man in the 22nd row who saw her not just as a sex object. And back then we thought Elton was straight, did we? We were such fools. Of course! *Smacks forehead* The clues were all there! The big camp ruffs, the poncing about like a dandy, the 'having bottom sex with other men'. The clues were all there.

3. Sorry, no. Not 'smuggling soldiers into Kensington Palace for sex' but 'Wings of Compassion'. I always get those two mixed up.

pram, simply had to grit his flamboyantly costumed teeth and get on with it.

Thus the biggest-selling single of all time to date,[4] the rewritten 'Candle in the Wind' for Diana, wasn't ever supposed to have been written or sung at all.

Thank Christ he didn't ask for 'The Bitch Is Back'.[5]

---

4. Sold 37 million copies around the world.

5. Or 'Saturday Night's Alright (For Driving)'. Or 'Goodbye Yellow Brick Road, Hello French-Built Brick Pillar', or any number of other poor taste 'joke' song titles that we all made up in the pub at the time. Tsk. How immature.

Pete Townshend Strikes Again?
(Or Rather, His Cat Does)

It's that man again. Not content with disfiguring porcelain[1] with cereal, the Who guitarist and occasional saver of teenage children from cancer[2] was once being interviewed for a special feature in a music magazine. With the interview over and the article in the throes of preparation, the great man gave the magazine's picture editor a box of personal photographs with the words 'I've got this load of photographs and if you like you

---

1. See 'The Best to You Each Morning' in this book somewhere.

2. The Who regularly save children from cancer with their regular Teenage Cancer Trust gigs.

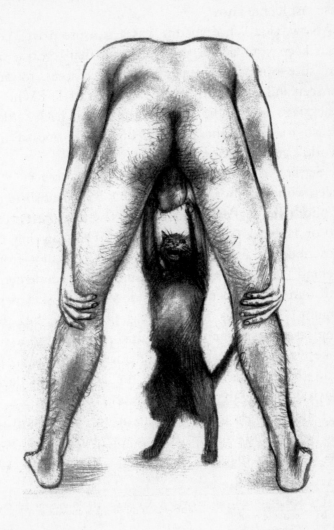

can go through it and if there's anything you want to use just let me know.'

Now, to a Who fan this was a treasure trove. You can keep your actual treasure trove that's got actual treasure in it because this was unlimited access to rare, unseen and indeed private photographs of The Who—backstage and candid. And lo, the joyous hack settled down to peruse the personal history of one of the world's greatest living beings.

Settling soon turned into unsettling, however, as deep within the box he found a 12 × 8 contact sheet of a photo shoot. Peering closely he saw that there were 10 or 12 black and white frames of what can only be described as a naked man bending over, shot from behind, with his admittedly impressive gentlemen's scrotum arrangement hanging down like a skin pendulum.[3] Now this in itself was unnerving, but the unpleasant-tasting cherry on this particular gone-off cake was that beneath the gentleman's legs was a cat. And the cat was reaching up on its two back legs, playfully batting the ballsack back and forth.

I should stress at this point, to protect the identity of the person concerned,[4] that there was, and is, absolutely no evidence that the photograph, testicles or cat

---

3. There was, apparently, no face visible. We can safely assume though that the balls were the model's own.

4. And, indeed, the identity of the cat.

belonged to Pete Townshend. I know Mr. Townshend has had his fair share of personal problems over the years but there should be no suggestion, implied or otherwise, that any of these problems ever involved either testicles, a cat, or both.[5] I merely bring the story to your attention. I suggest that those wishing to pursue this matter further should contact Mr. Townshend[6] directly and arrange an appointment to examine his scrotum for scratch marks and/or traces of Whiskas Kitten.

Needless to say, the photograph wasn't used in the article.

---

5. Yes, I know the title of this story suggests that it *was* his cat. But, if anyone asks, I am happy to say that it wasn't. All I know is that it was in a box of his photographs. Beyond that you're on your own.

6. Or his lawyers.

Dinner for Three

Who are the two most miserable people in music? Morrissey, perhaps, with his penchant for singing only vegetarian songs and waving daffodils about like a floppy-haired gay Alan Titchmarsh. Or what about Jimmy Nail when he wakes up each morning and remembers 'Crocodile Shoes'?

Well, uhUhhh *makes buzzer off Family Fortunes noise*, because it's neither of those. It is of course Van Morrison and Bob Dylan, who between them, according to those around them, could suck the joy from even the happiest of rooms like a soul Hoover.

So imagine the fun when they went out for dinner

together. It transpires that Van 'The Man' Morrison and Bob 'The Other Man' Dylan used to share an accountant[1] and at one point in the 70s, when the great men happened to be in London at the same time, this mutual acquaintance and holder of the key to their fortunes invited them both for dinner at his favorite restaurant. What a nice idea. No, really, that's a nice gesture, isn't it? You are a bridge between two of the world's greatest recording artists and decide to buy them dinner in a first-class restaurant, where you can perhaps sit back and be party to the meeting of these great musical minds as they relax off duty in the company of an excellent menu and fine wines. And then, when they both accept your invitation, you are flattered and thrilled because at the end of the day you are an accountant and therefore your life is only one step away, in terms of interesting, from that of a single-celled organism.[2]

So anyway, the evening arrives, you get dressed in your most non-accountancy-looking suit and toddle off to the restaurant to meet the two giants of rock and

1. They still might. I don't know. I haven't researched this fully because there was a deadline looming and *Spooks* was on.

2. Of course, this doesn't apply to my accountant. No way. Absolutely no way. And nor to the Inland Revenue. They're brilliant. Really brilliant. I've made nothing from this book, you know. Nothing. No need to come looking. You carry on doing that fantastic job you do somewhere else. Move along, nothing to see here.

crazy roll. You arrive at the same time as they do, you all take your seats and then . . . they utter not a single word to each other. All night. Nothing. Not. One. Word. The meal is served, the wine is poured, the evening drags on and on over course after course after course[3] and still the two men say not one word to each other. And neither do they say a word to their considerably uncomfortable host. In fact any and all of his attempts at making small talk simply evaporate into the air like the ghost of a fart and float away on an ill wind of awkward silence.

Time dragged on. Eventually, Bob Dylan looked at his watch and left. When he'd gone Van Morrison leaned across the table and spoke to his host for the first time that night: 'I thought Bob was in pretty good form tonight, didn't you?' he said.

I imagine the bill was claimed as expenses.

---

3. This is a posh restaurant. None of your Harvester or Angus Steak House for these boys.

Johnny B. Bad

Yes! He's back! Of course he is. It was inevitable because the other story in this book about Chuck Berry[1] failed to mention the time he was arrested for putting hidden cameras in a ladies' toilet. Chuck owned the Southern Air restaurant in Wentzville, Missouri. If we're being specific[2] it was at 1102 Pitman Avenue and was quite popular with the locals who patronized it. It was part of Berry's complex of properties that were known as Berry Park and he often received female visitors and guests, who were free to use his dressing

---

[1]. See 'Chuck Up' in this book. It's the story involving a dressing room, a blowjob and a sandwich, a service Pret A Manger are sadly lacking.

[2]. Which we are.

rooms, bedroom and facilities when they visited. And now we know why. It was because Chuck wanted videotape of their mimsies.

It was 1990 and Chuck was sued by 200 women who alleged that one of the most celebrated bluesmen ever to come out of the South[3] had used hidden cameras to secretly videotape them as they undressed and/or used the toilet either in his home or at his restaurant. The charges were 'invasion of privacy' and 'intrusion on their seclusion and privacy', which is more or less the same thing and is essentially legal speak for 'wanting videotape of their mimsies'. So there was suing, raids on Chuck's home[4] and court appearances. Then there was countersuing,[5] arguing, counterarguing, more raids, more court appearances and then the restaurant closed.[6] In the end all charges were dropped.

---

3. Well, that's where Chuck himself claims to hail from. Official records say California.

4. Which uncovered drugs and guns and a videotape of nudey girls. Oh come on. We've all done it.

5. 'My client maintains that all and any mimsies on his property are for personal use. My client is not, nor has he ever been, a mimsy dealer. He alleges that the mimsies in question were planted by the police'—actual transcript from the trial, 1990.

6. Missed a trick there. Should have reopened it after the trial and called it 'Mimsies'. That's a great name for a restaurant; 'Come to Mimsies. We've got fine home cooking and vaginas.' What? Oh come on, it's no worse than Bill Wyman's Sticky Fingers.

On November 6, 1990, Chuck complained that even though he was innocent, the fact that he'd been charged at all meant that his career had stalled. But far from it. In fact what he'd done is invent *Big Brother*. Fast-forward ten years and a toileting mimsy was prime-time TV with upwards of 5 million viewers. Chuck, you're still a pioneer.

Ryder on the Storm

Ah, the sun-kissed island of Jersey. Mostly famous for *Bergerac* and putting out for the Nazis. Oh, and being home to people who don't pay income tax. And potatoes.[1] But it was also where, after a Happy Mondays gig circa early 90s, the band's unintelligible, drug-drizzled lead shouter, Shaun Ryder, was detained in a Jersey police cell for a night at Her Majesty's pleasure for transgressing the island's strict 'substances' law,

---

1. 'From Charlie Hungerford's evidence, Chief Inspector Barney Crozier, we can conclude that Detective-Sergeant Jim Bergerac is a tax-dodging Nazi potato botherer. Take him away.'

being in possession, as he apparently was, of something illegal.[2]

By this time the Mondays were surfing the crest of their twisted melon-y fame wave (incidents such as the Newcastle City Hall/Simply Red interface long since behind them[3]) and so the very next morning, sitting in his cell and no doubt reflecting on his foolish behavior, Shaun was pleased to discover that the Mondays' manager, Nathan McGough,[4] had arrived at the police station. Stepping into the alcohol-perfumed cell, Nathan duly assuaged Shaun's worries and told him that he would be out soon, as the record company were in the process of 'getting him an advocate'.

Shaun stared at him for a moment as this information fought its way into confused ears, down befuddled nerve endings and attempted to decode itself somewhere in the fog of Shaun's bewildered brain. Slowly the cogs, cogs blunted by the pressures and temptations of rock stardom, began to turn and at last Shaun turned his baleful eyes toward his mentor and spoke: 'Leave it out, Nathan, you cunt. I'm in a lot of trouble here,

---

2. We don't know exactly what, but I think it's fairly safe to assume it wasn't a pirate DVD of *Beauty and the Beast*.

3. See 'Simply the Bezst', in this actual book.

4. Managed the band from 1988 and got them their first written contract from Factory Records. So technically the Happy Mondays were all his fault.

what do I want with some puffy yellow southern drink?'

Shaun Ryder, we salute you.

Eatin' the Blues

They suggested we might as well 'Jump', were 'Hot for Teacher' and, perhaps less famously, had 'Unlawful Carnal Knowledge', but whatever they did one story will always buzz around Van Halen like a lost wasp. Called 'Van Halen' after Eddie and Alex Van Halen at a time when it was cool to name your rock band after yourself,[1] the be-Lycra'd boys from California used to

---

[1]. See also Bon Jovi. And less successfully, Winger. However, it by no means always works. Just imagine: The Darkness might have been called 'Hawkins', Muse could've been 'Bellamy' and Def Leppard would've been called 'Fat Bloke from Sheffield Squashed into Leather Trousers'.

include one of rock's most bizarre requests on their tour rider: they would simply ask for a bowl of M&Ms with the blue ones[2] taken out. And then if, by the time they arrived at a venue, this wish hadn't been complied with, they'd simply refuse to play.

So was this arrogance? Self-importance? Up their own arseness? Not a bit of it. It was simply their way of testing how much attention to detail a promoter had paid to their requests. For instance, if a venue had gone to the trouble of sorting and excluding various small sweets in terms of their color then the band could reasonably assume that the other important technical requirements had also been adhered to. However, if their bowl of M&Ms was still awash with the rogue blue, or worse, if there were no M&Ms at all, then it stood to reason that corners may well have been cut elsewhere. It was basically a litmus test of sweets.

It was an excellent idea and it caught on. Nowadays Jamie Cullum won't go *near* a jazz piano unless he gets a box of Mingles, k. d. lang won't do anything without a chocolate lesbian and Pete Doherty won't even put his stupid hat on unless he gets a great big Easter egg full of heroin.

Good work, Van Halen.

---

2. Some say it was the brown ones. Doesn't matter. The point remains.

Ozzy Osbourne and the
Exploding Mouse

And now it's time for another Ozzy Osbourne tale. The notorious live bat incident[1] had recently passed and, in the face of an outcry from animal rights groups, Ozzy had weathered the resulting media storm and

---

1. The one where he bit its head off. Actually that sounds like a good title for an episode of *Friends*: 'The One Where He Bit Its Head Off'. Ross and Joey discover a headless torso in Monica's freezer and suspect Chandler of being the serial killer who is conducting attacks on the homeless of New York. Their worst fears are confirmed when Rachel comes home early to find him gnawing on the severed leg of an Ugly Naked Guy that he's killed and dragged back to their apartment. She is horrified. Doubly so because there's blood on Monica's best tablecloth. Meanwhile Phoebe is a bit 'kooky'.

was continuing with his tour. Notoriety was follow-ing him where'er he did roam and he'd put up with protests outside venues, criticism from all sides and even a rabies injection,[2] so when he saw a mouse in the middle of the stage midway through his concert packed with metal fans the last thing he wanted to do was draw attention to it, or, God forbid, accidentally stand on it.

The mouse was frightened and trapped with no-where to go and Ozzy's heart went out to the poor creature. So, even though he was in mid-song, he subtly attempted to attract the attention of a roadie offstage. It took some time. The song was coming to an end as Ozzy managed to catch the roadie's eye and subtly gesture toward the poor, terrified rodent. The roadie struggled to understand[3] but, with Ozzy still singing and hoping the crowd hadn't spotted it lest they bay for its mousy blood, he finally saw what Ozzy was pointing at. Looking back at Ozzy he could see that the great man clearly wanted something done about it.

And so it was that, perfectly in time with the end of the song, the audience was treated not to a display of pyrotechnics but the sight of a six-foot hairy roadie

---

2. What do you mean, you don't know the story? Everyone does. Fan throws bat onto stage. Ozzy thinks it's rubber. Ozzy picks it up. Ozzy bites its head off. It's a real bat.

3. He was a roadie.

in shorts running onstage and booting a mouse high
above the crowd, where it hit a light and exploded.

Tsk. Mice, eh?

He'll Be Coming Round the Mountain

Time now for a recipe for disaster. In the very early morning, take one out-of-it and not-slept-all-night Roy Harper and Jimmy Page and add one mountain. Then take a small film crew and drop in a plan to record the hairy legends playing an acoustic version of Harper's 'Me and My Woman', on a hillside, for broadcast on BBC2's whispery music show *The Old Grey Whistle Test*.[1] Stir until thoroughly mixed up.

---

1. This session was filmed on November 6, 1984. According to led-zepplin.com they also recorded versions of 'Same Old Rock' and 'Hangman'.

So, as Ralph McTell never said, let me take you by the hand and lead you to the Peak District sometime in 1984. The plan is to climb England's highest peak, Scafell Pike,[2] early in the misty morn and shoot the piece against a background of a mysterious mountain. The first thing then is that Jimmy ignores the 5 a.m. wake-up call to his hotel room. This is because he hasn't been to bed yet and thus doesn't technically need to wake up. Instead of getting slumberous respite from the tribulations of being a Rock God, Mr. Page has chosen to stay up all night imbibing a cocktail of hotel minibar miniatures, a somewhat powdery 'sharpener' and a young female acquaintance of unknown origin.[3]

After rousing an equally bleary-bearded Roy Harper and much banging on Jimmy's door, the film crew finally prize Page away from the pleasures of the flesh and, with Roy and Jim's faces as craggy as the mountain they're about to climb, they set off. There's the cameraman, the sound man, the director and producer along with Roy and Jimmy and their entourage, which consisted solely of Jimmy's young female acquaintance and

---

2. I was forced onto this mountain as a child. It was up there with the holidays in Wales for me. All I remember is rain and my dad's *AA Guide to Country Walks* breaking apart into wet, pulpy chunks.

3. Hmmm. When I went to Scafell Pike, aged eight, all I had was a fucking tent. And eight boxes of Ricicles from a Kellogg's Variety pack.*

* See 'The Best to You Each Morning' (in this book).

a handful of whiskey miniatures. Due to the condition of Mr. Page the climb is somewhat arduous and, anxious to keep the early-morning ethereal light, they soon choose a spot and begin to set up. The shoot was to be done on film and the rolls that the crew had were ten minutes long, so while Roy and Jimmy were sitting on a rock staring dizzily at the grass, it was politely explained that the version of 'Me and My Woman' they were doing should be a short one. They were handed their guitars and the camera began to roll. Nine minutes and 30 seconds later they still hadn't reached the chorus. The director called, 'Cut', explained to the boys that the ten-minute rule wasn't a joke but a fact and could they please try to concentrate because they needed the song, start to finish, to fit exactly on one roll of film. Roy and Jimmy continued staring at the grass.

The camera rolled again. It was then that Jimmy got up, mumbling something about 'going for a piss'. The camera stopped. Jimmy wandered over to a nearby drystone wall with some sheep[4] on the other side, taking his hitherto spectating young female acquaintance with him. Without words he indicated that she should help him with his ablutions. The camera began

---

4. Another story tells of Roy Harper contracting a particularly nasty and vicious strain of anthrax, reputedly after giving a sheep the kiss of life. I have no idea if this incident took place on this very same trip to Cumbria, but I like to think that it did. Possibly as a result of trying to save the sheep from drowning in a pool of the Led Zep guitarist's urine.

to roll again.[5] She then undid his trousers and took out his penis. There then followed a fantastic few moments where she, with the practiced skill of a veteran, directed the piss of Page, hoselike, wherever and at whatever he indicated, including the wall, the sheep, a bush, herself and finally his shoes. When he was sated, she shook him dry and tucked it back inside his leather trousers. They wandered back, Jimmy picked up his guitar and he and Roy performed an awesome version of 'Me and My Woman' start to finish, note-perfect, within the allotted time.

Jimmy Page, we would like to shake your hand. Hand. I said hand.

---

5. Cameramen should always be prepared. It is exactly this kind of professionalism and ability to capture creatures in the wild that David Attenborough relies on. Sadly, the film, much like Jimmy we hope, has since been wiped.

One Final KISS

It's them again. And this is quite possibly my favorite KISS story. They're onstage somewhere big. It doesn't matter where. They're half an hour into the gig, the stadium is rocking, the makeup is melting and the Lycra is sweating. '(I Wanna) Rock and Roll All Night'[1] has been dispensed with. 'Let's Put the "X" in Sex'[2] has lifted the roof off and 'Crazy Crazy Nights' has turned

---

1. And party ev-er-ry day.

2. Sample lyric: 'Love's like a muscle and you make me wanna flex'. Now that is excellent. Poetry in fact. You can take your Ivor Novello song-writing award and shove it up your arse.

262

this evening into exactly one of those. Oh yes, tonight, Kiss are rolling out the big guns.[3]

As they reach the climactic end of 'I Love It Loud' pyrotechnics devices explode, the lighting goes wild and the crowd screams louder than hell itself.

'Are you having a good time??' yells Gene Simmons.[4]

'Aaaargghhhh!' screech the 73,000-strong crowd of long-haired rockers, licking up every word.

'We're gonna do a big song for you now,' announces Gene, almost purring into the microphone.

'Aaaaargghh!' opine the crowd.

'Are you ready for another???' he asks them with a mighty rock yell.

'Aaaaarghhh!' they don't hesitate to reply.

'What's the second song off the *Destroyer* album?' he screams at them.

' "King of the Night Time World!" ' they scream right back to him, as one, without hesitation. There is a pause.

Then another pause.

Then another.

Then Gene speaks again: 'OK. What's the *first* song off the *Destroyer* album?'

---

3. Not literally. Although, come to think of it, they may have done it. AC/DC certainly did.

4. Rumored to have the longest tongue in rock. In fact, in anything. Including cows and lizards.

' "Detroit Rock City!" ' they shout back.

Gene leans his makeup-strewn face to the sky and thunder rumbles off his tongue: 'That's right. This is "Detroit Rock City".'

Endpiece

If you've enjoyed this book, or even if you haven't, why not send your rock 'n' roll rumors to the author via the website www.statusquoandthekangaroo.com? You never know, there might be a volume two, providing this one has sold more than eight copies. I'm sorry we can't return any of your edited stories because we send them to Tony Hart,[1] who likes to scrunch them up to make a collage.

---

1. Unless he's dead. Can't be arsed to check.

Further Reading

The Status Quo and the Kangaroo Code
Rosemary Conley's Step-by-Step Low-Fat Kangaroo Cookbook
Cracking the Status Quode
Eats, Status Quo and the Kangaroo and Leaves
The Status Quo and the Kangaroo Delusion
Status Quo and the Kangaroo According to Jeremy Clarkson
The Dangerous Book for Kangaroos

All available now.

Acknowledgments

I am indebted to the following sources of many a fine tale . . .

John Baker, Andrew Collins, Trevor Dann, Roger Drew, Dave Henderson, Stuart Maconie, Iain Martin, Joel Morris, Ozzy Osbourne, John Pidgeon, Paul Putner, David Quantick, David Whitehead, various anonymous webmongs at various anonymous gossip websites and all those who, wittingly or unwittingly, provided me with the aprocryphals herein. Thanks also to all the DJs, pop stars, road crew, journalists and music industry executives who were happy to talk and then happier to talk even more when I got them drunk and told them I'd leave their names out. You know who you are and what you drank. A million thanks also to all at Michael Joseph and Penguin, especially Rowland White, Carly Cook and Anwen Hoosen and to Vivienne Clore and all at the Richard Stone Partnership.

Double thanks to Roger for the illustrations. If anyone can convincingly draw a cat batting a man's testicles, he can.

Most of all, thanks to Nicki for the idea.